The
Border Guide

The Border Guide

Written by:
Robert Keats

Published by:
The Ontario Motorist Publishing Company
1253 Ouellette Avenue, Windsor, Ontario
N8X 1J3
Printed in Canada

ISBN 1-895654-07-6. 3rd revised edition, 1994
(ISBN 1-895654-05-X. 2nd revised edition, 1993)
(ISBN 1-895654-04-1. 1st edtion, 1992)

Contents

Chapter Four

YOU STILL CAN'T TAKE IT WITH YOU

Chapter Five

DOCTOR IN THE HOUSE

Chapter Six

TAKE THE MONEY AND RUN

Chapter Seven

COMING TO AMERICA

Chapter Eight

THE GRASS IS ALWAYS GREENER

Chapter Nine

GIVE MY REGARDS TO WALL STREET

Chapter Ten

TAKING CARE OF BUSINESS

Chapter Eleven

IN GOD WE TRUST

DEDICATION

This book is dedicated to my late father Gordon Keats,
(1922-1992). May he rest in peace with our heavenly Father.

ACKNOWLEDGEMENTS

No man is an island. This book could not have been possible without the assistance of many people. I have been blessed with a lovely family; my wife Barbara and my children Sarah, Daniel, Carl and the newborn baby Rebekah, who have been my inspiration. My only regret in writing this book was the time I had to spend away from them all.

The research required to prepare any book of this scope is enormous, even under ideal circumstances. Taking highly technical topics such as immigration, tax planning, and estate planning between Canada and the United States, and presenting them in a format that is both logical and readable, has been a particularly formidable task. I would like to acknowledge Tom Connelly, my partner of six years for providing a great deal of the material for the chapters on investments and currency speculation.

Anna Ochoa Thorne, a Harvard graduate, and a Phoenix immigration attorney, supplied much of the technical expertise and reviewed all of the immigration issues presented in Chapter 7. I thank her for both her time and prudent counsel.

The vast majority of this book was conceived and written in a wonderful little cabin nestled among the tall pines of northern Arizona. I would like to thank Teresa Bertocchi, a long-time family friend, for the use of her cabin. I will never forget the fresh mountain air, the spectacular thunderstorms and the warmth of the fireplace. A special thanks to Robin Ingle and Nomad Travel Insurance for providing me with much of the material included in Chapter 5.

I would also like to thank all of you who read the first and second editions of this book, for your positive comments and enthusiastic support. My final and biggest thank you goes to all of our cross-border Canadian clients. Without their interest and encouragement, I would have never been in a position to write this book.

ABOUT THE AUTHOR

ROBERT KEATS, CFP, RFP

R obert Keats, is an internationally known expert in cross-border financial planning. His views on how Canadians can better manage their financial affairs have been featured on CTV National News, the Financial Post and other international media. He is the publisher of *The Sunbelt Canadian* newsletter, and a financial columnist for *The Sun Times*, a Florida based newspaper for Canadians.

Besides writing and conducting workshops, Keats is also the founding partner of Keats, Connelly & Associates, in Phoenix, Az., the only U.S. based firm to specialize in cross-border planning.

Keats began his financial planning career in 1976, after retiring as a Captain in the Canadian Armed Forces. A graduate of the University of Manitoba, he was one of the first U.S. planners to earn a Master of Science degree in Financial Planning from the College of Financial Planning in Denver, Colorado. He is currently the only person in North America to hold the highest financial planning certification available in both the U.S. and Canada. (CFP and RFP)

Keats currently resides in Scottsdale, Arizona and his other interests include family, church and volunteer work.

PREFACE

Canadians make millions of visits to the United States every year. The Free Trade Treaty, and the Goods and Services Tax, fueled the fires of cross-border commerce, and many Canadians have migrated to the Sunbelt seeking temporary or permanent refuge from the harsh, northern winters.

Canadians tend to feel perfectly at home in the U.S., because the two nations' social and cultural institutions resemble one another so closely. Many incorrectly assume that the laws governing investment, taxation, and immigration are the same as well. Unfortunately, this assumption can lead to some unpleasant surprises, particularly when conducting basic financial transactions, such as buying, or selling American real estate.

The Border Guide has been written for Canadians who are considering some form of permanent or seasonal residency in the United States. It will also prove valuable to those of you who intend to invest, or do business in the U.S. This book may even prove useful to Canadian residents whose curiosity about the United States is limited to an occasional shopping trip or vacation. Whatever your interest, the information contained in these pages, will help you to transact your cross-border business affairs, with competence, and with confidence. It is the first step-by-step guidebook for Canadians who want to understand and take advantage of U.S. and Canadian tax, financial, and medical institutions. It will also show you how to avoid many of the common pitfalls of having assets, and spending extended periods of time in both countries.

In order to prevent this book from becoming the type of dry technical manual that is factually accurate, but functionally useless, we have presented our ideas in a non-technical fashion. Certain concepts have occasionally been simplified in the service of readability. Sound professional advice is also recommended for the application of any of the ideas or techniques detailed in this manual.

CHAPTER ONE

CROSSING
THE BORDER

AN INTRODUCTION TO PERSONAL
CROSS-BORDER FINANCIAL PLANNING

A s the economic and tax environment between the United States and Canada grows in complexity, the need for comprehensive personal cross-border financial planning becomes more and more necessary. The intent of such planning is to capitalize on the most satisfactory mix of savings plans, insurance coverages, investment vehicles, tax strategies, retirement plans and estate planning techniques available in each country. Applied to your own specific needs and goals, these cross-border planning opportunities can reap great financial rewards for you and your heirs.

Cross-border financial planning encompasses all the basic individual financial planning requirements of both Canada and the United States, in the areas of net worth, cash flow, risk management, retirement goals, taxation, estate planning and investments. It analyzes each area according to your particular situation, and then weighs option against option, completes timely currency conversions, factors in your immigration status, examines applicable tax treaty rules, and develops a road map for you to follow, to achieve your financial goals with maximum income, safety and tax savings.

One of the major difficulties inherent in cross-border financial planning, is that the rules change depending on immigration status. For example, a winter visitor to the United States marrying a United States resident dramatically alters his or her financial planning options, and a new cross-border financial plan becomes necessary in order to take advantage of new opportunities and avoid any mistakes. Figure 1.1 lists all the major immigration status options. All of the important planning issues for each respective status category, are discussed in detail, in subsequent chapters of this book.

HOW LONG CAN YOU REMAIN IN THE U.S. AS A VISITOR?

Few things cause more confusion and controversy among winter visitors than how long they can legally remain in the United States without breaking any rules. The source of this confusion is primarily due to the fact, that there are at least four sets of rules

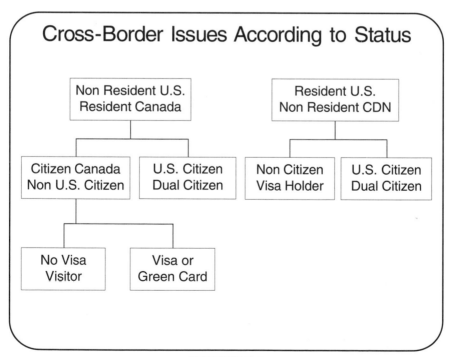

FIGURE 1.1

governed by different government agencies, that deal with residency. These residency rules sometimes conflict, and adherence to one set of rules does not automatically mean compliance with the others. The four sets of rules that tell you how much time you can legally spend in the United States are listed as follows:

1. **The Immigration Rules.** Canadian visitors to the United States may enter the country without any actual visa being issued. Technically, they fall into the B-2 visitor category (or B-1 for those entering for business purposes) allowing them to legally remain in the U.S. for up to six consecutive months. Extensions to the six month limit, primarily for medical reasons, may be granted by the Immigration and Naturalization Service (INS). However, the easiest way to extend this visitor limitation, is to simply leave the United States and re-enter at any border crossing including those between Mexico and the U.S. The six month clock starts over again each time you enter the United States. You will, however, be stopped from re-entering the country, if it appears that you have taken up permanent residency, and may be asked to show proof you have not. Proof that you have not become a United States resident can be whatever the immigration official at the border decides, but will likely include simple things such as your last three months utility bills, a provincial drivers license, or a property tax notice. Chapter 7 provides further direction for those Canadian visitors who wish to become permanent residents of the United States.

2. **The Income Tax Rules.** Generally speaking, a person will be classified as a U.S. resident for tax purposes, if he or she is present in the country for more than four months each year under the "substantial presence test" detailed in Chapter 3. *Note that the number of days present in the U.S. need not be consecutive. An individual can be deemed a resident of the United States for tax purposes, although they may not have any right to remain in the country under the immigration rules.* Thus, a person may become subject to income tax in the United States on their world income, without having the

right to remain legally within its borders for more than six months as a visitor. Consequently, it is much easier to become a resident of the United States for tax purposes, than to become a permanent resident under immigration rules as explained in Chapter 7. It is also possible to be a resident for tax purposes, of both Canada and the United States, at the same time.

3. **The Estate Tax Rules.** What estate tax is, and how it applies to non-residents is covered in detail in Chapter 4 and in Chapter 8 for U.S. residents. Unlike income and immigration, there is no clear set of rules of residency for estate taxes, as there is for income tax and immigration. Instead, it is based on a series of facts and circumstances. Some of the factors that determine residency or "domicile" for estate tax purposes are: The relative size and nature of your permanent homes in Canada and the United States, the amount of time spent in each country, written declarations on such documents as wills or tax returns, the locations of your significant assets and important papers, personal, family and business connections. Generally, Canadians who clearly visit the United States, and whose intent is to routinely return to Canada each year could not be considered to have given up domicile in Canada, and would not be subject to American estate tax on their world-wide assets. Court cases, where the IRS has challenged a Canadian winter visitor's estate, by attempting to tax world-wide assets of the deceased, have failed. The IRS was unsuccessful in those cases, because there must be a clear intent to give up one domicile for another. Visitors to the U.S. however, may still be subject to the non-resident estate tax on their U.S. located assets. This will be explained in greater detail in Chapter 4.

4. **The Provincial Medicare Rules.** These sets of rules are unique, because they act in direct opposition to the tax and immigration residency rules, by stipulating that you cannot be away from your home province for longer than a specified period of time. In 1991 Ontario, Quebec and Saskatchewan

have joined with the majority of Canadian provinces by requiring that you must normally be present in the province for a minimum of six months a year, and have a permanent residence available to you there to remain eligible for provincial medicare. Ontario's OHIP has even threatened to disqualify those Ontarians who reside in summer cottages or RV's, when they return from wintering in the Sunbelt. The amount of time included in the time out of province to potentially lose medicare also includes time spent in other Canadian provinces, as well as out of the country.

We have often been asked "How do the particular government departments responsible for enforcing any of the above rules, know how much, and where you are spending your time." The fact of the matter is, they do not always necessarily need to know. Instead, they pass the burden of proof on to you, by asking you to declare, under penalty of perjury, that the facts you present regarding your travel itinerary are true. Also be aware that we live in the computer age where information is easily stored and retrieved. This information is increasingly being shared by various government agencies and government owned corporations.

WHERE TO LIVE OR WINTER IN THE U.S.

Cross-border financial planning will vary according to which U.S. state you chose to live or vacation in. This guide is not meant to provide you with a visitor's bureau style brochure about which Sunbelt state is the best, but examines some of the major tax implications of the three most popular Sunbelt states: Arizona, California and Florida. In Appendix B, we will provide tax rates and other technical data on these, and other popular states. From both a climatic and amenity standpoint, the reasons why Arizona, California and Florida are so popular with Canadians, can be summarized in a collection of comments from long time residents or visitors to one or more of the three states:

5

Arizona

- Offers the most sunshine of almost any populated area in North America. Expect clear skies nearly 85% of the time, and an annual rainfall of 6 inches (15cm). Winter daytime temperatures range from 65° to 85°F (18° to 30°C) in the Phoenix and Tucson areas.

- Great for people with arthritis because of the dry climate. Not so good for allergy sufferers, since something is always in bloom.

- Golfers paradise. There are more than 120 golf courses in the Phoenix area alone that are open 365 days a year.

- Geographically diverse state from the Grand Canyon to mountain country to desert. There is decent snow skiing in northern parts of the state during winter, and plenty of year-round water sports on the numerous man-made reservoirs and lakes.

- The most often mentioned drawback about Arizona, is that if you chose to stay in the Phoenix area during the summer, you can face average daily high temperatures of over 100°F (38°C).

California

- Plenty of sun and ocean. Temperatures vary considerably from the coast to the inland desert, with the coastal areas having less extreme temperature changes because of the moderating effect of the Pacific Ocean. The Palm Springs area, has a climate almost identical to that of southern Arizona.

- Major man-made and natural tourist attractions abound, such as Disneyland, Hollywood and Big Sur.

- The ocean provides plenty of opportunity for sailing, fishing and whale watching.

- Geographically diverse state from the miles of spectacular coastlines to the mountains, farmland, vineyards and desert.

- The major drawback of this state is its population, which is more that of all of Canada, causing gridlock on the freeways, and a great deal of pollution. Because Palm Springs lies next to a major fault, many Canadian visitors got shaken by the earthquakes in the spring of 1992. California also is noted for its high cost of living and relatively high taxes.

Florida

- Very mild climate with a minimal range between winter to summer temperatures, 70° to 90°F (20° to 32°C) on average. Expect plenty of rain year round, and high humidity during summer.

- Provides two surprisingly different coasts, the Atlantic and the Gulf. Each has miles of beautiful beaches, islands and keys and all the year-round water sports that go with them.

- Like California, major man-made tourist attractions such as Disney World and Cape Kennedy are located there.

- Florida has no personal income tax.

- It is easy to get to Florida by car from Ontario, Quebec and the Maritimes.

- This state offers the most services for Canadians. It has several radio and TV stations broadcasting Canadian news in both French and English. In addition, it has several major Canadian weekly newspapers.

- The major complaint about Florida seems to be that it is too crowded, particularly on the Atlantic coast, and its high humidity and hurricane season.

POPULAR CROSS-BORDER MISCONCEPTIONS

This book, in addition to acting as a guide, will help dispel many of the popular misconceptions about living, visiting and investing in the United States. Some of the more common misconceptions are:

- *You lose money changing Canadian dollars to U.S. dollars!*

No, there is no loss exchanging one currency for another, other than the commissions you pay as a transaction cost. You don't make a profit changing U.S. dollars to Canadian dollars either.

See Chapter 2 for a more complete explanation of this popular misconception.

- *Canada has no estate or inheritance taxes!*

  Wrong, Canada's deemed disposition tax on death on RRSP's or RRIF's and appreciated property can be as high as 53%. Many provinces also levy significant probate fees. For smaller estates Canadian estate taxes are frequently much higher than those in the U.S. See Chapters 4 and 8 for further details on this tax.

- *RRSP's can be left alone if you move to the U.S.!*

  Leaving your RRSP's in Canada when you move to the U.S. can create many potentially costly tax problems, and you may miss opportunities to withdraw them at no, or very low tax rates.

  Chapter 8 discusses how to remove your RRSP free from net income tax, once you have taken up residence in the U.S.

- *You will earn lower rates of interest investing in the U.S.!*

  It is true that most Canadian banks pay higher interest rates than U.S. banks on deposits. However, overall diversified investment portfolios earn about the same rate of return, for a similar level of risk in both Canada and the U.S. Chapters 6 and 9 provide further insight into this misconception.

- *Wills are all you need for a complete estate plan!*

  Wills are very necessary, but there are more effective estate planning vehicles like living trusts and living wills, that may provide for less estate settlement costs and better estate management. See Chapters 4 and 8 for a further explanation.

- *Investing in the U.S. means you must file U.S. tax returns!*

  No, there are a large number of investments that you can invest in the U.S. that are exempt from taxes and any filing or reporting requirements. Chapter 6 lists the investments that are exempt from U.S. taxes for non-residents.

- *You can't be a citizen of Canada and the U.S. at the same time!*

  Wrong, dual citizenship is possible, and has been for several years. Chapter 7 explains dual citizenship status.

- *You lose your CPP and OAS by moving to the U.S.!*

  No, you keep all these benefits, and in reality you will likely keep much more of your CPP and OAS after taxes once you have become a resident taxpayer of the United States. Chapter 8 provides the calculations to show you some of the tax savings available on CPP and OAS when a Canadian moves to the U.S.

- *Medical insurance is too expensive in the U.S.!*

  Some U.S. health insurance is expensive, however those under 65 can obtain very good coverage with high deductibles for less than $100 per month for up to a $1,000,000 limit of coverage. Those over 65 are usually eligible for U.S. Medicare, at no, or reasonable costs. Chapters 5 and 9 provide further details for those needing health insurance in the U.S.

- *Investments in the U.S. are riskier than in Canada!*

  No, the same rules of prudent investing apply in both countries. Because there are more investment choices in the U.S., there can be greater opportunity for an inappropriate investment to be chosen. This greater selection also allows prudent investors to find a larger number of safe U.S. investments.

WHAT IS THE CANADA - U.S. TAX TREATY?

One of the most important documents for the protection of a Canadian's financial assets in the United States is the Canada — U.S. Tax Treaty. However, most Canadians are unaware of its existence, and the benefits it provides them. Even though tax planning is an important part of cross-border planning, it is our experience that few financial advisors have ever cracked the cover of this treaty on behalf of their clients. They tend to focus instead, on the tax rules of their own individual countries.

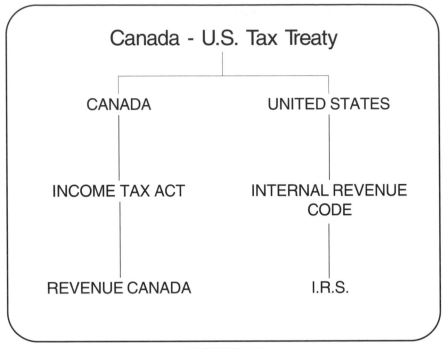

FIGURE 1.2

Canada and the United States signed their first full tax treaty in 1942, with subsequent amendments in 1950, 1956, 1966 and 1980. The most recent amendment was written in 1980, and became effective in 1984. It is undoubtedly, the most important tax treaty for both Canada and the United States. Millions of Canadians and Americans are affected by this agreement, and as Canada and the United States continue as each other's major trading partner, its impact will increase.

The Canada — U.S. Tax Treaty attempts to accomplish the same goals as any tax treaty: The prevention of tax measures that may discourage trade and investment, reaching a common ground on the taxation of non-residents to avoid double taxation on the same income, and to protect the domestic treasury. To a large extent the Canada — U.S. Tax Treaty has accomplished these goals. However, changes in domestic tax rules, in the area of non-resident estate tax in the United States, which took effect in 1988, have prompted a new round of treaty negotiations beginning in 1989, that are currently ongoing. The two countries are attempting to negotiate an estate tax article to the existing treaty, which will resolve the high potential non-resident estate tax, and/or capital gains tax Canadians face when holding United States real estate and stocks. The U.S. non-resident estate tax will be covered in greater detail in Chapter 4.

Up until now, Canadian winter visitors have been able to use the Canada — U.S. Tax Treaty protection by default, without having to make any active filings or declarations. Current regulations now require that formal statements be filed with the Internal Revenue Service (IRS) forcing Canadians who spend four to six months in the U.S., to become more aware of the treaty, and how it can help them, if they do not wish to be taxed on their world income in both the United States and Canada. Chapter 3 has been designed to show you who must file returns or statements in the United States, and under what circumstances.

The Canada — U.S. Tax Treaty is one of the most important tools used in cross-border financial planning for two key reasons:

• The terms of the treaty take precedence over almost all the Canadian Income Tax Act (ITA) and the Internal Revenue Code (IRC) tax rules in the United States.

• The terms of the treaty seldom change. The Canada—U.S. Tax Treaty has been amended only four times in its 50 year history and can be relied on to a much greater degree than either the Canadian ITA or the American IRC, which are subject to constant revision without notice, and the effects of annual budgets, bipartisan politics and election campaigns.

11

THE VALUE
OF A BUCK

HOW TO BEAT THE
EXCHANGE RATE BLUES

R egular visitors planning their annual winter migration to the American Sunbelt, frequently display symptoms of confusion, helplessness and insomnia, just prior to leaving the country. This highly contagious phenomenon is known as the Exchange Rate Blues. A general feeling of malaise develops when the soon to be departed snowbird starts calling the banks or poring over the financial pages of the daily papers. This is done in an often futile attempt to pick the best possible moment to convert their hard earned Canadian dollars into American currency. Questions like "should I wait until _____" (fill in the blank with an appropriate response such as: tomorrow, next week, until the Bank of Canada sets its rate, or the exchange rate goes up another cent, etc.) feverishly run though the mind of a traveller infected with the Exchange Rate Blues. Finally, the deal is struck and the currency exchanged, but the very next day the Exchange Rate Blues continue when new symptoms known as the "I should ofs" appear. "I should of waited until _____" (again fill in the blank with the appropriate response like "when the exchange rate improved," or if it went the other way, "I should of changed more.")

I have spoken to literally thousands of Canadians in the United States, and every one of them including myself have experienced the Exchange Rate Blues at one time or another. The vast majority of Canadian winter visitors usually feel the symptoms around August.

ELIMINATING THE EXCHANGE RATE BLUES

Most winter visitors would never dream of becoming a currency speculator to make money for their retirement because of the high risks. *However, going through the annual guessing game of which way the Canadian dollar is going, is precisely that; currency speculation.* In fact, it is this unwitting currency speculation that is the root cause of the Exchange Rate Blues. The Exchange Rate Blues by the way, is very similar to the feeling novice commodity traders go through every time they make a trade.

How do you avoid currency speculation, and the Exchange Rate Blues? *The answer is very simple. Place enough income producing assets in U.S. dollar generating investments, to produce sufficient income to safely cover your expenses during your stays in the United States.* This is simply a variant of the time-honored tradition of not putting all of your eggs in one basket. You will be diversified against currency risk, and hedged against rapid fluctuations in either currency. The Exchange Rate Blues will become part of your past. In addition, you'll also save those extra dollars in commissions that financial institutions build into their exchange rates. These commission are particularly high when small sums are exchanged. To determine the rate of commission, compare the rate listed in the financial sections of the newspaper, with that posted at your bank or at the airport on the same day. It can be as high as 3% or more.

HEDGING YOUR BETS

Currency hedging is practiced by almost every large corporation conducting any kind of cross-border business. For example, a Canadian airline knows that next year, it is going to have to pay for that new Boeing 747, it will move to protect itself from adverse currency fluctuations. It will either generate more United States income from

13

its assets, or purchase a currency futures contract locking in the current U.S. dollar rate in effect an insurance policy that they will enjoy the current exchange rate or better, one year from now when the jet must be paid for. Failure to hedge or reduce their currency risk exposure in this situation, could mean the airline might pay millions more, based solely on fluctuations in the Canadian dollar.

If you're a typical Canadian winter visitor, who expects to be spending part of their retirement south of the border, you will require large amounts of U.S. funds. For example, if you are currently age 65, and wish to maximize your time in the sunny south, you would need at least $180,000 US, in today's dollars, to fund 15 years of stays, for six months a year. If you, in fact do not protect yourself, or hedge your currency risk, like the Canadian airline in the above example, your retirement in the United States could end up costing you thousands of dollars more.

Figure 2.1 show the year end Canadian dollar values, as expressed in U.S. funds since 1975.

Figure 2.2 shows how the purchasing power of a Canadian winter visitor with $100,000 CDN invested in 1975, has fared, assuming they earned an average 10% return each year in Canada, and then converted the annual interest into U.S. funds to finance their stay in the Sunbelt. Figure 2.2 identifies this person as the Speculator. Compare this with the Planner, shown on the same chart, who converted their $100,000 CDN in one lump sum in 1975, and invested it at the same rate of interest in the United States, and then covered their U.S. expenses from the interest earned.

From Figure 2.2, you can see that the Planner, who decided not to speculate where the Canadian dollar was going, came out much farther ahead than the Speculator, who kept their $100,000 income earning investment in Canada, and then kept going through the annual Exchange Rate Blues. The Canadian who failed to hedge against the currency risks of the Canadian dollar, took a voluntary pay cut on their retirement investment income of over $33,361 or 20% including additional exchange commissions calculated in at 1.0% per year. In addition, the Speculator's original principal balance has been reduced from $100,000 US to only $75,500 US, and they lost the opportunity cost of earning interest on the $33,361 they lost over the years. This lost opportunity cost adds another $43,861 to their losses, making a total loss of $101,610 in a 18 year period! Could this happen to you? Even though it may not have worked out well during the past seventeen years, speculating on the Canadian dollar can be profitable, if you feel lucky. *If you want to have a secure retirement however, avoid the Exchange Rate Blues, and don't become a currency speculator.*

EXCHANGE LOSS IF YOU CONVERT CANADIAN DOLLARS NOW

Investing a large lump sum of your savings in the United States is a way to avoid the Exchange Rate Blues and protect yourself from currency risk. The major concern and usual first comment of nearly every client that we recommend this strategy to, is "How can I exchange my dollars now, I will take too much of a loss." *The real*

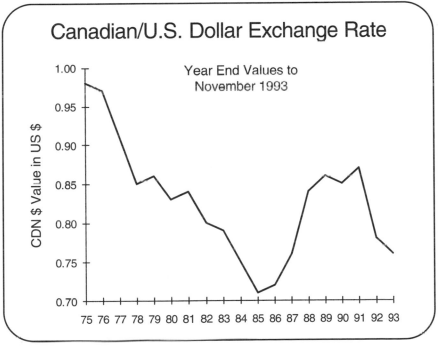

FIGURE 2.1

truth is there is no loss at the time you convert Canadian dollars to U.S. dollars.

To illustrate this point, Figure 2.3 shows that $1,000 CDN exchanged into foreign currency, would net you $750 in US dollars, $5,845 Hong Kong dollars, L 1,198,400 Italian lira or 2.1 oz. of gold. We are assuming that you would pay no exchange rate commissions and all transactions transpired at the same time.

Would you consider it a gain because you changed $1,000 CDN to $5,845 Hong Kong dollars? Or, would you consider yourself a millionaire because your $1,000 CDN bought you over 1,198,400 Italian lira? Of course not. Why, should someone think they had lost any money because their $1,000 CDN bought them only $750 US?

Figure 2.3 also illustrates that it doesn't matter what currency you are using, or whether it is denominated in dollars, lire or something else. It takes the same relative amount of each currency

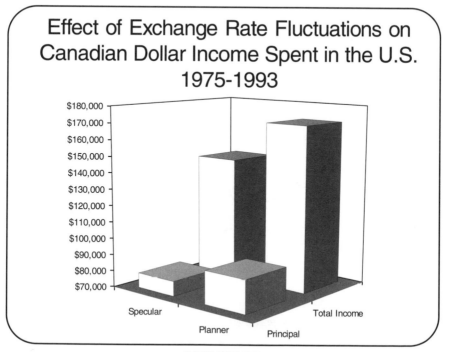

FIGURE 2.2

to purchase the same tangible object such as the 2.1 oz. of gold used in this chart. Instead of gold you could easily substitute, a months rental on a United States vacation property and the net result would be the same. To further illustrate that there is no loss or gain on currency exchange transactions, run through a full cycle of exchange from $1,000 CDN to L 1,198,400 Italian lira to 2.1 oz. of gold, to $750 US back to $1,000 CDN. There is no loss at any time of the currency exchange. Losses or gains can occur only if you repeated this full cycle of exchange, at some other point in time. As time passes, the relative values of the four currencies and the gold will change and trying to guess what those future relative values will be, is pure speculation.

The only loss when exchanging Canadian dollars to U.S. funds is that which is perceived, and not a real one. This misconception comes from the close proximity between the U.S. and Canada, and the fact that both countries call their currency the dollar. Adding to

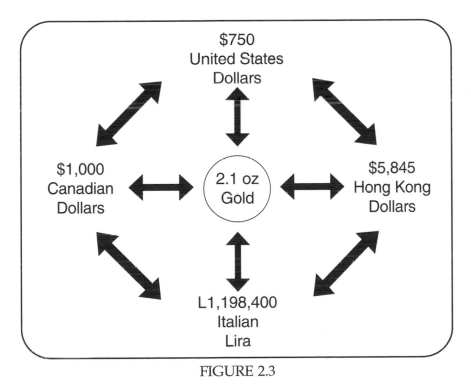

FIGURE 2.3

this misconception, is that at one time (approximately 20 years ago) one dollar Canadian was worth approximately one dollar U.S. There is no law or agreement, written or otherwise, that states that the Canadian dollar must be worth one dollar U.S. for any reason whatsoever. The relationship between the Canadian dollar and the United States dollar is market driven, based on world-wide demand, and is every bit as unrestrained as the relative values of the Canadian dollar and the Italian lira. Had the United States called their currency francs, or something different like zlotnays, this perception of loss would not likely have ever occurred.

WHAT CAN YOU EXPECT IF YOU INVEST IN THE UNITED STATES?

Interest rates on bank term deposits, GIC's and government bonds in Canada have historically been higher than the same relative rates in the United States. Consequently, Canadians tend to avoid investing in the United States because they feel they can get better returns in Canada. This need not be true however, if you follow prudent investment practices and keep a proper balance in your portfolio, no matter how big or small it is. *The main reason for higher Canadian interest rates is that the world market perceives greater risk in Canadian currency, and that risk must be compensated for, or global investors will not invest in Canada.*

We live in a world economy today, and your investments need to be administered as if you were operating a business, and managed it on a world-wide basis. If the business of your investments is managed correctly, you will earn the same level of profit or income at the same relative risk whether you are in the United States or Canada.

For example, compare a mutual fund in Canada to one in the United States with the same objectives, restrictions, management and fee structure, and over time, you will see that their returns will also be similar on a percentage basis. The only difference is that one generates Canadian funds, and the other generates U.S. funds.

As a result, you do not have to take any reduction in income and can maintain the same level of safety, by directing some or all of your investments to the United States. This effectively avoids speculation on the Canadian dollar, and will cure the Exchange Rate Blues.

AVOIDING U.S. INCOME TAX ON YOUR INVESTMENTS

Investing in the United States as a non-resident can be rewarding and worry free, if you follow the same investment principles you would use in Canada, and then stick with those investments which are exempt from both American income and estate tax. There is no substitute for diversification and good management, regardless of what your investment objectives are. Chapter 6 lists those investments which Canadians can use, to produce a steady U.S. income, while avoiding the non-residents estate tax discussed in Chapter 4. *The fact that these investments are exempt from tax and reporting requirements in the United States does not mean that you don't have to report the income to Revenue Canada. As a Canadian resident, you are subject to tax on your world income in Canada.*

WHERE IS THE BEST PLACE TO EXCHANGE MONEY?

As most experienced travelers will tell you, the rates of currency exchange can vary dramatically, depending on the form of your Canadian dollars e.g. cash, cheque or travelers cheques, and the facility you are using to make the exchange, i.e. a bank, brokerage firm or airport. Whether you are in Canada or the United States will also be a factor in obtaining the best exchange rates.

World currency markets dictate exchange rates based on many constantly changing factors. It is primarily the commission rates that vary between exchange rate vendors. Obtaining the lowest commission rate will be the focus of our attention here.

There is no exact formula that will guarantee you the best rate of exchange each time, but the basic guidelines listed below, will save you plenty of dollars in exchange commissions.

- Exchange large sums at one time, whenever possible.

- When exchanging at banks ask for the "spot" rate. This is the special rate right from the market at that time. This service is generally only available when exchanging amounts over $5,000 or more.

- Avoid using Canadian cash for the exchange. Commission rates on cash can go over 5%. Cheques and travelers cheques generally attract the best rates. Personal cheques work fine only at a bank where you are known.

- Shop around at least three or more institutions giving each vendor the exact amount you are exchanging, and the form the Canadian dollars will be in at the exchange. If you are going to use a bank, include both United States and Canadian banks in your survey. You may get some pleasant surprises if you do. There are now several U.S. banks and brokerage firms in Florida that are exchanging Canadian dollars at greatly reduced commission rates to attract new customers.

- The Custom House Currency Exchange, based out of Vancouver, guarantees that their exchange rates will beat any bank every time. In our dealing with them we have found that it is true they make the Canada - U.S. dollar exchanges at far better rates than any bank or brokerage firm for that matter and they don't try to sell you something. They are easy to work with regardless of where you are, including the U.S., through their toll free number 1-800-661-3559.

- If you have a relationship with a brokerage firm you can generally exchange money there at no, or very low commissions. They are of course, hoping that you will invest the money through them.

- If you are in one of the major gambling cities like Las Vegas, the Casinos tend to offer excellent rates of exchange. They may frown upon you however, if you do not stop to gamble some of your newly acquired U.S. currency before you leave.

- Credit card companies generally offer a preferred exchange rate when you use their charge card to purchase foreign goods. They also charge high interest rates on the purchases, if you are not back in Canada, or have not made other arrangements to pay the bill when it's due.

THE TAXMAN COMETH

CROSS-BORDER TAX PLANNING

I n Chapter 1, we alluded to the fact that cross-border financial planning can be very beneficial for all those who undertake it diligently, and can be very costly to those who ignore it. The key areas, in terms of providing the best return on your investment of time and money, come in the areas of income tax, and non-resident estate tax planning. This chapter will deal with the income tax issues, while Chapter 4 will delve into the non-resident estate tax.

Figure 1.1 in Chapter 1, lists the various cross-border issues according to your immigration status in the United States. Most of these issues deal with income tax. The first category that we will examine, is the typical winter visitor, who spends less than six months a year in the U.S. and have no visa, or other immigration status in the United States.

TAXING NON-RESIDENT ALIENS

Non-residents, or non-resident Aliens as the U.S. tax and immigration publications like to refer to them, are generally taxed on their U.S. source income only. Income from U.S. sources includes interest on bonds, notes and other interest bearing obligations, all wages for services performed in the United States, dividends, rents, royalties and the gains from sale of property. The Canada — U.S. Tax Treaty sets forth the withholding rates, if any, on these sources of income.

The treaty withholding rate is 15% on interest. *The IRS has taken a position not to collect the treaty withholding tax on interest from all U.S. Banks, Savings and Loans and similar institutions providing the non-resident has filed an IRS Form W-8 with the payer of the interest.* Form W-8 is the certification of foreign status and entitles you to this withholding exemption. Most banks keep a good supply of W-8 Forms or they can easily be obtained from any IRS office.

Non-residents earning dividends in the U.S. will face a 15% withholding rate, reduced from 30% by the Canada — U.S. Tax Treaty. Canadians may have to file IRS Form 1001, Reduce Rate Certificate, to ensure they get the treaty rate of withholding rather than the regular rate.

Gains on the sale of U.S. securities are exempt from United States capital gains tax, providing you have filed a W-8 form with your broker.

Canadians collecting rent have two options; either pay a flat 30% withholding tax on the gross rent, or file a non-resident tax return, Form 1040NR, netting expenses against the rent and then pay regular tax rates on the net rental income at the applicable rate. Most Canadians with rental income will find that they will pay less tax, and perhaps no tax at all, if they file a U.S. return. *Even if you clearly made no profit from your rental property and paid no withholding tax, you must still file a Form 1040NR, unless you enjoy playing Russian Roulette with the IRS.* New IRS regulations have been enacted that will disallow any rental expenses 16 months after the normal filing deadline of June 15, each year. If the IRS catches up with you for failure to file, you would then be forced to pay tax and penalties on the gross rent collected.

Canadians selling real estate will be exempt from withholding tax if they are selling their personal use residence, if it is under $300,000 in value, and the buyer is going to occupy the home for his own personal use. Otherwise, the withholding rate is 10%, whether or not there will be any profit on the sale. Application can be made to the IRS to reduce or eliminate the withholding tax, if there is only a small gain or a loss on the sale of the property. The gross amount of the sale transaction is reported to the IRS on Form 1099-S and the details of any gains or losses must be reported to the IRS on Form 1040NR, for the year of the sale. If there is further tax to be paid on a gain it will be paid with this return and likewise, if there is a refund due of any withholding, this is the mechanism for applying for it. Canadians who owned their property prior to 1980, the date of the new Canada — U.S. Tax Treaty, may use the treaty to exempt any gains prior to December 31, 1984, from taxation in the U.S.

Remember that exemptions from U.S. tax on any of the afore-mentioned income, does not mean that it is exempt from Canadian taxation. A Canadian resident is taxable on their world income.

Most Canadians investing to produce United States income will have no U.S. withholding tax to pay, or tax returns to file if they use the exempt investments first mentioned in Chapter 2 and explained in detail in Chapter 6. The section headed *Who Must File U.S. Tax Returns* later in this chapter, will tell you exactly under what circumstances, and when you must file a non-resident tax return.

DUAL CITIZENS & GREEN CARD HOLDERS RESIDENT IN CANADA

Canada taxes its citizens on their world income, only when they are residents of Canada. The United States taxes its citizens and resident aliens or Green Card holders on their world income, with certain exclusions, regardless of where they reside in the world.

There are many Canadians who have obtained United States Green Cards over the years, when they were handed out more liberally than they are today. Some Canadians have never used these Green Cards to become residents of the United States, while others have used them but moved back to Canada to set up principal residence there. Chapter 7 deals with the immigration implications of a Canadian in this situation. From a tax stand point, the IRS considers all Green Card holders as legal permanent residents of the United States, and subject to the same filing requirements as anyone else with resident status. That is, they must file annual tax returns in the United States on their world income. There can be numerous tax advantages of paying taxes in the United States rather than Canada, and these are covered later in this chapter, and in Chapter 8. *However, Canadians in this situation, need to determine as soon as possible, whether they should officially abandon their Green Card or use it to their best advantage.* The best means to make the final decision about what to do in this situation, is to complete a full cross-border financial plan that addresses every issue, from the perspective of getting the best of both the Canadian and United States systems. If you do nothing, and continue to sit in the woods with your Green Card, you may end up getting the worst of both systems, instead of the best.

Canadians who were born in the United States, or obtained U.S. citizenship from some other source (see Chapter 7, *Derivative Citizenship and Dual-Citizenship*) and who are also naturalized Canadian citizens, are dual-citizens of Canada and the United States. Dual-citizens living in Canada are in a similar situation tax wise to the Green Card holders described above. They need to file annual tax returns in both countries on their world income. *Similarly, Canadians who are dual-citizens need to determine, as soon as possible, whether they should officially abandon their U.S. Citizenship, or use it to their best advantage.* Our advice here, is also the same. Complete a cross-border financial plan and use it to position your dual citizenship to obtain the best advantages between Canada and the United States. Chapters 8 and 9 will give you some general guidance as to what your options are.

IRS GIVES CANADIANS AMNESTY

Canadian residents who are holding U.S. green cards, U.S. citizens, dual citizens and derivative U.S. citizens who have not been filing U.S. annual tax returns on their world income have been given a window of opportunity to come out of the closet and get back on the correct U.S. filing roles without penalty. The amnesty program requires simply that the last six years tax returns be accurately filed with the international section of the IRS in Philadelphia and then correct returns be filed on a continuing basis in the future by the required deadlines. If the past six years returns are filed the with IRS will waive basic penalties (but not interest) on tax due, if any, and reduce the normally unlimited stature of limitations for failure to file to the same six years by not asking any questions as to what happened to any income or taxes due prior to the six years.

The requirement to file in the U.S. on world income does not necessarily mean that there would be taxes due to the U.S. on income earned in Canada. There are exemptions such as the earned income exemption of $75,000 US providing it was not U.S. sourced income. In addition to this employment income exemption, the Canada/U.S. Tax treaty allows for foreign tax credits for taxes paid in Canada on the U.S. return on the same income. Since Canadian tax rates have been significantly higher than U.S. rates in recent years the foreign tax credits from taxes paid to Canada usually would cover any U.S. taxes due. However, there are certain circumstances where U.S. taxes can be due on income that would not be taxed currently if the taxpayer/U.S. citizen was filing only in Canada. For example, if a U.S. citizen in Canada had a capital gain on some stocks or mutual funds in Canada that qualified for the $100,000 capital gains exemption they may be exempt from tax in Canada but since the U.S. has no equivalent exemption they would pay tax to the U.S. at the standard U.S. capital gains rate. A similar problem can arise when a Canadian resident/U.S. citizen takes advantage of the Canadian principal residence exemption in Canada since the U.S. principal exemption works quite differently. U.S. citizens in Canada taking dividends from their closely held Canadian corporations in an attempt to zero out Canadian tax with the dividend tax credit could also find themselves paying U.S. taxes on the dividends received. If a U.S. citizen resident in Canada has an RRSP, the IRS will consider interest, dividends, and capital gains earned in the RRSP income unless an election provided by the Canada/U.S. Tax Treaty is filed to defer the tax each year with the

U.S. return (see Chapter 8 the withdraw your RRSP Tax Free section). One can correctly surmise that the IRS regulations requiring U.S. citizens to file annual returns, in light of the differences in the applications of tax rules between Canada, can provide for some very potentially unpleasant surprises. This amnesty program can be of great advantage to any U.S. citizen to get back into the good graces of the IRS and to avoid penalties or to prevent the IRS from ever scrutinizing any financial transactions prior to the six years of required returns that may have required large amounts of U.S. taxes to be paid. Failure to take advantage of the amnesty program may be a costly mistake. The IRS is now tracking passport renewals and travel visa requests by U.S. citizens and has an active campaign to find and prosecute non-filers around the world. So if a U.S. citizen in Canada who has not been filing the required U.S. returns continues to do so without taking advantage of the amnesty program they may find themselves eventually facing costly penalties and being forced to file U.S. returns for more than six years once the IRS eventually catches up to them. The IRS may not even find their non-filers until an estate tax return filed at the death of the taxpayer which is when they tend to audit more closely causing the estate to pay potentially large enough penalties, interest and taxes to reduce an inheritance to zero.

As a consequence, U.S. citizens in Canada require constant cross-border tax advice to avoid unnecessary tax and construct a plan that takes advantage of the best of U.S. and Canadian tax systems while at the same time avoids the pitfalls. Proper planning from a knowledgeable cross-border planner can turn these apparent tax problems into great tax saving opportunities. U.S. green card holders in Canada, in addition to needing to follow the same tax rules as U.S. citizens in Canada, face the added concern that they would lose their green cards since filing U.S. tax returns is one of the key indicators that the residency rules required to maintain the green card are being followed.

As of the printing of this edition of the Border Guide this amnesty program was open but the IRS may at any time lift the program so anyone wishing to use this program needs to check with their cross-border advisor to see if it is still available and if not, pursue other alternatives like negotiation to get current with the IRS without penalty.

NON-RESIDENT TO A RESIDENT IN THE U.S.

Canadians who regularly spend less than four months a year in the United States, do not have to worry about becoming a resident of the United States for tax purposes. They will keep themselves void of any filing requirements other than the situations listed later in this chapter under the section heading *Who Must File in the U.S.*

From Chapter 1 under the section *How Long Can You Stay in the U.S. as a Visitor.* you may recall there are different sets of rules that apply to winter visitors, such as being considered a U.S. resident for tax purposes and yet having no right to remain in the United States as an immigrant. This section will examine the tax rules that make this apparent contradiction possible.

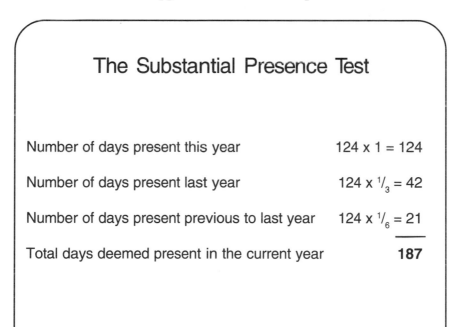

The Substantial Presence Test

Number of days present this year	$124 \times 1 = 124$
Number of days present last year	$124 \times \frac{1}{3} = 42$
Number of days present previous to last year	$124 \times \frac{1}{6} = 21$
Total days deemed present in the current year	**187**

FIGURE 3.1

Substantial Presence Test. A winter visitor is considered to be a resident of the United States for tax purposes, if they meet the substantial presence test. The winter visitor satisfies this test if they have been present in the U.S. for at least 183 days during a three year period that includes the "current year." The current year is the particular tax year for which the winter visitor is determining their resident status. For purposes of the substantial presence test, a winter visitor will be treated as "present" in the U.S. on any day that he or she is physically present in the U.S. at any time during the day. This would include any cross-border trips you make to the United States being counted as a full day, even if you were present in the United States for only a few hours. Note that the days present in the U.S. need not be consecutive.

Each day of presence in the first preceding year, is counted as one-third of a day and each day of presence in the second preceding year is counted as one-sixth of a day. For example, Figure 3.1 illustrates the results of these calculations for a winter visitor who spends four months in the U.S., plus a few cross-border shopping days in the adjoining border town. Even though this winter visitor never came close to spending six months in the United States, they can be deemed to have spent 187 days in the current year, and are therefore a United States resident for tax purposes under the substantial presence test.

In computing the days of presence in the U.S. under the final rule, certain days are not considered as days of presence. These include any day that an individual is prevented from leaving the U.S. because of a medical condition that arose while the visitor was in the U.S.

If an individual is not physically present for more than 30 days during the current year, the substantial presence test will not apply even if the three-year total is 183 or more days.

Closer Connection Exception. A winter visitor who meets the substantial presence test, may nevertheless be considered a non-resident alien for the current year if they: (1) are present in the U.S. for fewer than 183 days during the current year; (2) maintain a "tax home" in a foreign country during the year; and (3) during the current year have a "closer connection" to the foreign country where they have a tax home other than in the U.S.

A tax home is considered to be located at the visitor's regular or principal place of business. If the individual has no regular place of business because of the nature of their business, or because the individual is not engaged in any business, the visitor's tax home is their regular place of abode "in a real and substantial sense." The tax home maintained must be in existence for the entire current year.

A visitor will be considered to have a closer connection to a foreign country, if the individual or the IRS establishes that the visitor has maintained more "significant contacts" with the other country than with the U.S. factors to be considered in determining, this include the location of the visitor's home, family, personal belongings, routine banking activities, and organizations to which the visitor belongs. Also, the closer connection exception is unavailable to a visitor who has taken steps to change their status to permanent residence during the current year.

TAX TREATY PROTECTION FROM TAXATION FOR NON-RESIDENTS

The Canada — U.S. Tax Treaty affords all Canadian visitors a great deal of protection from filing in the United States and paying taxes on income not sourced in the United States. In addition, that income which is effectively sourced in the United States, is prevented from being double taxed; once in the United States, and again in Canada. The treaty accomplishes this in three key ways:

1. **Foreign Tax Credits.** The treaty allows for a system of credits such that tax paid to one country on specified income, will be allowed as a full credit against any tax due on that same income in the country of residence. For example, a non-resident who earns a taxable rental income in the United States, files and pays tax as required by the IRS. The tax paid to the IRS is converted to Canadian funds and is used on the Canadian return as a full credit, to reduce or eliminate any Canadian taxes due to Revenue Canada on that same rental income.

To: Internal Revenue Service Center
Philadelphia, PA
19255

Exemption Statement 1993

From: Name: _____
Address: _____
City: _____
State: _____, Zip Code: _____

RE: Nonresident Alien Closer Connection Exception

To Whom it May Concern:

I, _____, do hereby file for the Closer Connection Exception for the 1993 tax year as per Dept. of Treasury, Internal Revenue Service, Regulations 301.7701(b)-2 & 301.7701(b)-3 and Publication 519 because:

(a) I was present in the U.S.: ____ days during the calendar year 1991.
____ days during the calendar year 1992.
____ days during the calendar year 1993.

(b) I was present in the United States fewer than 183 days in the 1993 calendar year: Yes ☐ No ☐.

(c) I maintain and reside in a permanent furnished residence at _____ in the city of _____, in the province of _____, Canada on which I pay property and school taxes to the City of _____.

(d) I have a passport from _____ (Passport # _____).
I do not have a Passport ☐.

(e) I pay Canadian Federal and _____ Provincial Income Taxes each year.

(f) I hold a valid Province of _____ Drivers Licence which expires on _____.

(g) I receive $_____ of my gross income from the conduct of business in the U.S. in 1993.

(h) I am a member of the congregation of _____ in the city of _____.

(i) I do my personal banking in Canada at _____.

(j) I vote in the Canadian Federal Election, in the Province of _____ election, and the City of _____ civic elections.

(k) I have not applied for or taken steps to apply for, permanent resident status during 1993 and have no applications pending for adjustment of status to that of a permanent resident.

I declare above statements to be correct and true.
They are made under penalty of perjury.

Signed _____ Date _____

FIGURE 3.2

2. **Exemptions.** The Canada — U.S. Tax Treaty provides for certain exemptions from filing or reporting income of a non-resident in the United States, that would otherwise be taxable by the IRS. The Substantial Presence Test, without any treaty protection, would apply to a large number of Canadian winter visitors who regularly spend four to six months each year in the American Sunbelt. Under the Canada — U.S. Tax Treaty, there is an exemption from the Substantial Presence Test for Canadians who without the treaty protection would be required to report their world income in the United States under the terms of this test. *New IRS rules to be implemented for the 1992 tax year, will require Canadians who are using the Canada — U.S. Tax Treaty as protection from the substantial presence test, to file an exemption statement (see figure 3.2) or Form 1040NR declaring they are treaty exempt.*

3. **Withholding Rates.** Provisions in the treaty establish the amount of maximum withholding either country can take on various forms of income. These withholding rates were detailed earlier in this chapter under the *Taxing Non-Resident Aliens* section. The provisions for maximum withholding rates prove very useful when doing cross-border financial planning, as you will see in Chapters 8 and 9.

The exchange of information capabilities between Canada and the United States as provided for in the Canada - United States Tax Treaty, can trap those who do not report income earned in one country to the other, where applicable. The Canada and U.S. tax authorities can currently ask for and obtain a complete tax profile of anyone they choose who lives in the other respective country at anytime. There have been some indications that a new Canada - U.S. Tax Treaty will contain provisions to enforce the tax judgement from one country in the jurisdiction of the other. This is currently not possible so if a tax payer owes tax to one country but lives in the other it is difficult for the country owed the tax to collect it unless they can find assets within the tax owed country to seize.

WHO MUST FILE IN THE UNITED STATES?

The purpose of this section is to make you aware of the situations and the types of income on which you are legally required to file a tax return of any form in the United States. You must file a return under the following circumstances:

- The sale of any United States real property requires that the seller file IRS Form 1040NR before June 15 following the year of the sale. Form 1040NR must be filed whether or not there was any gain or withholding tax collected on the sale. There are no exceptions to this rule.

- Any non-resident who spends four to six months per year in the United States, and is deemed to be a resident under the Substantial Presence Test, and who is claiming to be exempt under the Canada — U.S. Tax Treaty, must file Form 1040NR or the exemption statement (see Figure 3.2) by June 15 every year they are subject to the substantial presence test. Refer back to discussions about the *Substantial Presence Test* in previous sections of this chapter.

- Any Canadian who spends more than 183 days in the U.S. is considered a resident for tax purposes, and must file a regular U.S. tax return, Form 1040, declaring their world income. The treaty will be of little help in preventing world income from being taxed in the U.S., but will help to eliminate most, if not all, of the taxes due to the IRS. Canadians in this situation, should review Chapter 7 on Immigration, with a view to obtaining some status to reside permanently in the U.S., so they may take full advantage of the lower U.S. tax rates as outlined in the last section of this chapter.

- Any non-resident who collects rental income in the United States from any owned property including their own personal use home must file Form 1040NR by the required deadline, unless the leasee is withholding the 30% non-resident withholding tax on the gross rental income.

- Any non-resident who carries on a business of any form in the United States, must also file Form 1040NR regardless of whether or not that business is profitable. This filing requirement applies even though you may not have any legal immigration status to work in the United States.

- If a non-resident has had withholding tax withheld incorrectly or at an improper rate, they must file Form 1040NR for the year in which the error occurred if they wish to obtain a refund. Be sure to keep all the reporting slips that any withholding entity must provide you with. Generally, these would be 1042S, 1099 or 8288A slips which are similar to Canadian T-4 or T-5's. Lottery and gambling winnings are considered taxable income in the U.S. and are subject to non-resident withholding tax. If you hit a jackpot in Las Vegas, this filing method could make you an even bigger winner by giving you some or all of your withholding back. **Planning Tip for Gamblers**: Keep detailed daily records of both winnings and losses. The losses can be useful when filing for a refund of withholding tax from a jackpot. Without good records, the IRS will not allow an offset of losses against winnings. You must also be considered to be engaged in the business of gambling as a professional.

- The estate of a non-resident decedent that has a U.S. taxable estate of greater than $60,000 must file IRS Form 706NA within nine months of the death of the decedent. See Chapter 4 to determine the taxable estate of a non-resident.

- Any non-resident who gifts taxable U.S. property over $10,000 total in one year to any single person, or $100,000 to a spouse, is subject to U.S. gift tax and must file IRS Form 709NA the gift tax return, to pay any taxes due by April 15 after the year end in which the gift was made. The gift tax rates are equal to the estate tax rates. See Chapter 4 for a more complete discussion of gift taxes.

HOW & WHEN TO APPLY FOR A U.S. SOCIAL SECURITY NUMBER

Generally speaking, Canadians do not need to apply for a U.S. taxpayer identification number, commonly known as a Social Security Number (SSN). However, you will probably be asked for one every time you open a bank account, or conduct any other financial transaction in the United States. *A very typical but incorrect response for Canadians is to give their Canadian SIN number.* Doing so is not only illegal from the stand point of providing a false SSN, but it throws the IRS computers for a loop, because your SIN number may be the same as some American's SSN, or there may no record of it at all. When opening a bank or brokerage account demand the IRS Form W-8, Certificate of Foreign Status, and this will satisfy any legal tax reporting requirements. See the *Taxing Non-Resident Aliens* section, earlier in this chapter.

There is no real disadvantage to having an American SSN unless having another number to keep track of bothers you. A SSN can be a convenience to you in certain financial transactions, such as filing tax returns or selling property. It may also be to a person's advantage to have a taxpayer identification number, to obtain increased assurance the IRS has properly recorded certain facts that

CANADA - U.S. TAX RATES 1993

ONTARIO CANADA		FLORIDA UNITED STATES	
Taxable Income	**Tax Rate**	**Taxable Income**	**Tax Rate**
$29,590 or less	31%	*Married Filing Jointly*	
$29,591 - $59,180	45%	$35,800 or less	15%
$59,181 and over	53%	$35,801 - $86,500	28%
		$86,501 - $140,000	31%
		$140,001 - $250,000	36%
		$250,001 and over	40%

FIGURE 3.3

could be helpful in the future, such as tax losses which are permitted to be offset against future profits. In fact, the IRS will likely assign you a temporary SSN when you do file a tax return.

To obtain your own permanent number, you must go to any Social Security office in the United States, and complete Form SS-5. Obtaining a SSN without any immigration status can be difficult, unless you insist you need the number to file U.S. tax returns.

The only time you are really required to have a SSN if you are a non-resident, is when you are actively engaged in a business in the United States. Real estate rental can be considered a business. All residents of the U.S. are required to have a SSN.

CANADA - UNITED STATES INCOME TAX COMPARISON

There are two main issues to consider when it comes to the actual amount of tax you pay; the tax rates, and the income on which those rates are applied, called your taxable income. No comparison between Canada and the United States would be complete, without considering both these factors. Since there are fifty states and ten provinces, a detailed comparison of each state and each province is beyond the scope of this book. Appendix B includes the tax rates from all provinces and the key Sunbelt states. However, we will provide you with a guide to the major opportunities of cross-border financial planning. We will also compare the tax rates of Ontario and Florida, the two locations that generate the most winter visitor traffic (Quebec also accounts for a similar amount of visitors to Florida). Other provinces and state tax rates will vary somewhat from the Ontario and Florida tax numbers, but the trends will be the same. The states in the U.S., which do have a personal income tax, collect their tax on a separate return in the same manner as Quebec.

Figure 3.3 charts the tax rates and income brackets of Ontario and Florida. The rates shown are for 1993, and include all provincial and federal surtaxes. For the purpose of our comparison, we assume that the Canadian is married to a spouse who has too much income to qualify for the married exemption in Ontario, and that the Florida person is also married, and filing jointly with their spouse.

35

As you can see from Figure 3.3, a Florida taxpayer in the highest income bracket has a strong advantage over the Ontario taxpayer because the Florida tax rate is 13% lower than Ontario's and it takes a much larger income to reach the highest bracket in the U.S. On the same income stream, a high income earner would cut their total taxes by nearly 40%, if they had the choice of paying their taxes in Florida. Chapter 8 will show you some direct comparisons using actual cross-border tax situations, to provide a more complete picture for those considering permanent residence in the United States. Florida has no personal state income tax, so the rates reflect the actual United States federal tax rates. Appendix B compares the provincial tax rates with those of popular Sunbelt states.

As we previously noted, you must look at taxable income as well as the tax rate, to get a complete picture of the total taxes paid. Now, we will look at the deductions that reduce your gross income to your taxable income. This list of deductions is by no means a complete summary of all the deductions available in both Canada and the United States, but it does cover the major tax deductions that apply to a married couple on, or near retirement age.

• Personal Exemptions

Canada has converted the basic personal exemption of $6,456 to a non-refundable federal tax credit of $1098. The age exemption for those over 65, has been reduced to a tax credit of $592. For a spouse or a dependent with no income, there are credits available of $915 and $71, respectively. The benefits of credits are enhanced by the applicable provincial tax rates. For any Canadian above the lowest tax bracket in Figure 3.3, the old personal exemptions would have meant a greater net tax reduction than the current credits.

The United States has a standard deduction total of $6,200. If the taxpayer itemizes certain deductions rather than taking the standard deduction, a greater total deduction may be taken. Add $1,400 to the standard deduction, if you and your spouse are over age 65. Add another $2,350 for yourself and each dependent including your spouse, regardless of his or her income, for personal exemptions. The United States is much more liberal with their dependent deductions. You may claim adult children, grandchildren, parents

36

and other close relatives for whom you supply over 50% of their financial support. The basic personal exemptions are phased out for married persons with incomes between $162,700 to $285,200. Certain itemized deductions will also be reduced up to 80%, for incomes starting at $108,450 to $208,450.

• Pensions

Canada *has the $1,000 pension deduction converted to a nonrefundable federal tax credit of $170.* Old Age Security is taxed up to 100% due to a claw back starting at incomes exceeding $53,214.

The United States has no standard pension deduction, and allows a tax free return of contributions to contributory pension plans making these pensions partially tax free. United States social security payments are totally tax free, until a married couple's income exceeds $40,000, and then up to 85% of these benefits will be taxed at the regular tax rates. *Those in the highest tax brackets will pay a 34% maximum tax on social security payments.*

• Mortgage Interest and Property Taxes

Canada — these are not deductible in any amount.

United States — *mortgage interest and property taxes on up to two homes are fully deductible as an itemized deduction.* The definition of a residence could also include an RV or a yacht. Total mortgages on these residences cannot exceed $1,000,000.

• Provincial or State Income Taxes

Canada — provincial taxes cannot be taken as a deduction from federal taxes paid.

United States — *state and municipal taxes are deductible as an itemized deduction.*

• Earned Interest Deductions or Deferment

Canada — the $1,000 earned interest exclusion and the ability to defer interest in investment vehicles such as Canada Savings Bonds and annuities have both been eliminated for all Canadian taxpayers several years ago.

United States — *any amount of interest earned on certain municipal bonds is tax free on both the federal, and in most cases, the state level.* Interest on United States Savings Bonds or other federal government securities is tax free at the state level. *Any amount of interest, dividends or capital gains can be deferred as long as desired through the use of various forms of annuities.*

• Capital Gains Deductions

Canada has *a life time $100,000 capital gains exemption on gains from securities other than real estate* (this deduction was available for real estate prior to February 1992, and those who owned qualifying property before that date, have limited grandfathered rights to use the exemption for gains accumulated prior to this date). *Persons who own a qualified small business may obtain $400,000 in additional capital gains exemptions on the sale of the shares of their company.* All capital gains on the sale of a principal residence in Canada are tax free. After the Canadian taxpayer has used all of their capital gains exemptions, only 75% of remaining gains are taxable, making the maximum capital gains tax approximately 40%, depending on the province.

The United States has no equivalent to the Canadian capital gains exemption. Capital gains are taxed at a reduced rate, with a maximum federal rate of 28%. Congress in August 1993 reduced the maximum capital gains rate on certain qualified small businesses to 14%. *There is a lifetime capital gains exemption of $125,000 for those over 55, on the sale of their principal residence.* In addition, any gains on the sale of a principal residence can be rolled tax free into a new home. There is no capital gains tax on deemed dispositions at death, and beneficiaries receive appreciated property without any income tax due. However, some assets of larger estates may be subject to the estate tax. See Chapters 4 and 8 for more details.

• Medical Expenses

In Canada, medical expenses that exceed 3% of income are allowed by converting the deductible expenses to a non-refundable federal credit at the 17% computation.

In the United States, medical expenses that exceed 7.5% of adjusted gross income are deductible as an itemized deduction. Premiums paid for health insurance are included as a deductible medical expense.

• Registered Retirement Plans

Canadians with earned income, can contribute 18% of their last year's earnings to a maximum of $12,500 to an Registered Retirement Savings Plan (RRSP) each year. If you receive payments from a registered pension plan, and have a spouse under the age of 71, you can contribute up to $6,000 to their RRSP as a spousal contribution, in addition to your own plan contributions.

Americans with earned income can contribute up to the lesser of 100% of income or $2,000 to their own, or a spouses Individual Retirement Account (IRA) each year. There are numerous other related qualified plans that can allow contributions of up to 25% of income to a maximum of $30,000 per year, depending on your employment status.

• Charitable Donations

In Canada, donations to qualified Canadian charities, not exceeding 20% of income, are allowed by the non-refundable federal credit at the 17% computation for the first $250, and 29% for the remainder.

In the United States, donations to qualified charities, not exceeding 50% of income, are allowed as an itemized deduction.

• Miscellaneous Deductions

Canada - Union and professional dues, safety deposit box fees, RRSP administration fees, interest on funds borrowed for investment purposes, and fees for investment advice are deductible expenses.

United States - tax preparation fees*, vehicle licenses, property and casualty losses exceeding 10% of income, unreimbursed employment expenses, trustee fees*, safety deposit box fees*, interest on funds borrowed for investment purposes to the extent of portfolio income, IRA administration fees* and fees for investment advice* are deductible expenses. *(*denotes expenses that are totaled and deductible only to the extent the total exceeds 2% of adjusted gross income).*

The net effect of the differentials in tax rates and deductions between Canada and the U.S. can be best illustrated by example, or by an exact calculation based on your personal situation. Chapter 8 will provide some typical cross-border tax situations that will show you how the application of different tax rates to the same income source, can result in substantial net tax differences between the two tax systems.

CROSS-BORDER Q&A

Many of the issues covered in the preceding chapter of this book have already been touched upon in the *Cross Border Q & A* column which appears in *The Sun Times of Canada,* and the author's own newsletter *The Sunbelt Canadian.* A majority of these questions were posed by readers, who were looking for advice relating to their own specific problems or situations. At the end of this chapter, we have included some typical reader questions, along with our response, to better illustrate and flesh out the concepts presented in the chapter.

Does a Green Card have an Expiration Date?

My wife and I moved to Florida in 1991 on a permanent basis as retirees. My wife is a U.S. Citizen and I have a Green Card issued in 1953. I do not intend to work.

I returned to Canada in 1954, retaining my Green Card and filed Canadian income tax returns from 1954 to 1990. I will file a U.S. return for the year 1991, and subsequent years. I will not file a Canadian return. My questions are:

1. Is my Green Card still valid, or do I have to re-apply for another Green Card?

2. Do I apply in Tampa or do I have to go back to Toronto?

3. When I file my U.S. return, am I liable to be asked why I did not file a return since 1954 and if so, how do I answer? And

depending on the answer, will the Internal Revenue Service inform Immigration and Naturalization of my status?

4. Will I be able to apply for U.S. citizenship after three years?

— *Edward P., Venice, FL*

Since you did not surrender your Green Card, and it has no expiration date, it is technically still valid. However, you were supposed to surrender the Green Card in 1954 when you left the United States.

Your best bet is to tread softly with the Immigration and Naturalization Service for awhile, and just start using the Green Card again each time you cross the border. Now that you have a permanent Florida home, the Immigration and Naturalization Service will likely never bother you from this point forward.

The Internal Revenue Service may question you though, as to where all your tax returns were since 1954. If they do question you, your best answer would be to show the Internal Revenue Service that you filed in Canada and paid the higher Canadian tax rates, and you may be able to keep yourself out of hot water with them. If you hurry you can also take advantage of an amnesty program with the IRS which requires you file the last six years U.S. returns. You will pay no penalties but will pay the taxes due if any with interest for the six years. The IRS will forgive any taxes that may have been due prior to the six years. You do need three or more continuous years of U.S. residency before applying for U.S. citizenship.

Avoiding U.S. Estate Taxes

I am a Canadian citizen, and a resident of Canada. I own a property in Florida that is valued in excess of $100,000 US I would like to sell this property to my daughter so that no estate tax will be payable on my death.

This property has increased in value by about $50,000 since I purchased it. This transaction will take place in Canada between two Canadian citizens. I know I will have to pay a capital gains tax in Canada but what are my liabilities in the U.S. as far as capital gains?

— *Todd A. O., Montreal, PQ*

You would be subject to Canadian capital gains of $18,500 on this transaction. If you have not used your $100,000 capital gains exemption you could possibly avoid paying tax to Revenue Canada by selling it to your daughter.

Under the Canada — U.S. Tax Treaty, your first obligation for taxes on this sale, would be to the IRS. Since the property is in the U.S. you will be subject to U.S. tax on the gain in the year of the sale. A $50,000 gain would accrue a total tax bill in the U.S. of approximately $12,500. This U.S. tax paid will provide an offsetting foreign tax credit against the $18,500 due in Canada.

Consequently, if these numbers proved accurate, you would pay $12,500 tax to the IRS and an additional $6,000 ($18,500 minus $12,500) to Revenue Canada for a total of $18,500 US.

Your goal is avoidance of the U.S. non-resident estate tax, but your current U.S. non-resident estate tax liability on this specific property is only $13,000. Paying $18,500 at current tax rates to save $13,000 in estate tax at some point in the future seems economically self-defeating. Selling the property to your daughter does not eliminate the estate tax, it only transfers the tax obligation to her estate. If she were to predecease you, the tax would be paid at her death, and if you inherited the property back, it would be taxed a second time at your death.

You would likely be better off looking at alternatives other than selling your residence to your daughter. For example, if you are currently around the age of 60, take the money you would have paid in taxes and buy a single deposit no-load life insurance policy with your daughter named as beneficiary. This would provide her with as much as $100,000 in tax free death benefits, enough to pay any estate taxes several times over. If you decide to sell the property to a third party before your death, you can cash out the policy and get your money back with interest.

If you are uninsurable due to health or age, investing the $18,500 anywhere at 7% interest will double the amount over 10 years; enough to pay the estate tax. Just make sure the investment is exempt from U.S. estate tax.

The current tax treaty does not allow you to offset U.S. non-resident estate tax liability with a credit for Canadian capital gains taxes if you hold property until death in the United States.

The U.S. and Canada are currently negotiating an addendum to the treaty to effectively allow credits from an actual sale of the property. Until the new treaty solves this double tax exposure, your estate would be liable for both taxes.

Effects of Dual Citizenship

What effects would dual citizenship have on Canadian citizens regarding income tax, etc.

— Devlin O., Tampa, FL

Although your question is a short one, there are no short answers. There are a large number of tax issues which will need to be addressed if a Canadian becomes a dual citizen, including your country of residence, the size of your estate and the types of income you are receiving.

Probably, the first question you need to address is, why become a dual citizen? Unless you intend to reside in the United States more than six months a year and Canada less than six months, you will not likely benefit tax-wise by becoming a dual citizen and in fact, you may expose yourself to some unnecessary tax complications.

Canada taxes its citizens only when they are actual residents of Canada. United States citizens are taxed wherever they live in the world, with tax credits allowed against foreign taxes paid by the United States citizens in another country of residence. Consequently, if you become a dual citizen, and still intend to reside in Canada, you will be required to file tax returns in both countries on world income. Filing in both countries affords you no tax advantages since you will pay the Canadian tax rate and take a credit for those taxes paid on the United States return. Your total tax paid between the two countries, under most circumstances, will not be any greater, but why complicate your life unnecessarily?

The real tax advantages of dual citizenship come when you become a non-resident of Canada and are no longer subject to

Canadian tax rules. Depending on your sources and amounts of income, you can realistically cut your annual income tax bill in half or more, with good cross-border financial planning.

Under the Canada - United States Tax Treaty, you can be a dual citizen and maintain a lifestyle of winters in the United States Sunbelt and summers in Canada, without being subject to taxes in both countries. Consequently, dual citizens can arrange their financial affairs in such a way that they pay tax on their world income only in the United States. Once you have completed an exit tax return from Canada, your tax situation becomes much clearer. Canadian pension plans and old age security are 50% tax free, and you are not subject to any claw back. Taxes on RRSP's and RRIF's withdrawals drop to 15% or 25%, depending whether they are periodic or lump sum withdrawals. Canadian interest, dividend and corporate pensions are subject to a non-resident withholding tax of 15%. You can also take advantage of a large variety of tax free, tax deferred or tax sheltered investment options in the United States, to substantially reduce or eliminate any tax on investment income.

The tax advantages of becoming a dual citizen and paying your taxes in the United States need to be greater than the net cost of United States Medicare, approximately $3,600 US each per year, or less if you qualify for U.S. Social Security. In addition, there are many complex estate planning issues that need to be addressed before making the move to dual citizenship, particularly if you and your wife's total estate is over $1,600,000 CDN. Over this amount, United States estate taxes will have to be taken into account.

Because of the complexity of the issues involved with becoming a dual citizen, I don't recommend you attempt such a move without a written plan completed by a cross-border financial planner. Talking to an attorney or accountant in either or both countries may only give you a part of a much larger puzzle, and can be confusing, especially if they lack knowledge of the other country's systems.

Differences Between Canadian Citizens & Legal Residents

Are there any differences in the legal situation (in Canada or the U.S.A. as well) between legal residents of Canada, and Canadian nationals travelling and/or investing in the United States? Do the Canadian federal or provincial governments differentiate between these two categories other than during elections?

— Flora A., Largo, FL

You didn't say what situation you are in now so I will attempt to answer your question by reviewing the most likely scenarios.

Please note there is more than one set of rules from at least two United States government agencies that may apply to you, depending on what you are attempting to do; so sorting out what rules apply to your situation may be difficult.

The first set of rules to consider, are tax rules from the IRS in the United States. The IRS doesn't differentiate between legal residents of Canada and Canadian citizens, unless the legal Canadian resident happens to also be a United States citizen. Canada taxes its citizens only if they are residents of Canada. The United States taxes its citizens regardless of where they reside in the world. Non-residents of the United States investing in the United States have certain tax withholding and filing requirements they may be subject to, depending on what they are investing in, and what country they come from. There is a Canada — U.S. Tax Treaty that segregates Canadian residents and citizens from other non-resident investors in the United States, with respect to what withholding rates on investment income, and what tax credits are allowed.

Legal Canadian residents or Canadian citizens travelling in the United States are subject to essentially the same Immigration and Naturalization regulations. Canadians are allowed to visit the United States without formal visa requirements. However, there are rules that apply such that Canadians travelling in the United States are technically on a B-2 visitors visa, which lasts up to six months and can be renewed by simply re-entering the United States again, to start the six months over. If you are immigrating to the United States, then your status in Canada as a landed immigrant or a citizen does have some bearing on what status you may apply for in the United States.

Canadian federal or provincial governments do not generally have any separate tax rules that apply to Canadian landed immigrants or citizens. Under Revenue Canada rules, citizens and non-citizens, as residents of Canada, are taxed identically.

Withholding Tax Compliance on U.S. Rental Income

What options are available to Canadian owners/renters in Florida, who through ignorance, have failed to comply with the 30% withholding tax, and who wish to square themselves immediately with the Internal Revenue Service?

— *Rolf J.,Williamsburg, ON*

Your question is a very good one, and a situation we run into quite often. Anyone who rents out their United States property for longer than two (2) weeks per year, is subject to taxation on this income in both the United States (under the Internal Revenue Code) and Canada (under the Income Tax Act).

First, you must decide which of the two methods, explained below, is appropriate for you. The first method has the renter withhold 30% of the gross rental income received, and forward it to the IRS Service Center in Philadelphia, PA. The onus is on the renter to withhold the tax if you are a non-resident landlord, but the IRS will come after both the renter and the landlord, if the tax is not paid as required.

The second method is to make an election under Section 871 of the Internal Revenue Code to be taxed as effectively conducting business in the United States, and file annually a Form 1040NR tax return in the United States. On this return, expenses incurred to earn the rent such as property taxes, utilities, mortgage interest, travel, etc. and allowable personal exemptions, are taken as deductions to arrive at a net taxable income for non-resident United States tax purposes.

By filing Form 1040NR, the non-resident taxpayer will generally pay less tax. In fact, most people in this situation make little or no profit after all expenses have been deducted and therefore no tax is due. Even if you do have some net rental profit the tax rate after deducting personal exemptions of $2,350.00 starts at only 15%.

A husband and wife can split this income on separate United States returns, and both take personal exemptions if the rental property was purchased jointly.

The forms for filing a return, the Form 1040NR and the necessary rental income Schedule E, may be found at any IRS office or may be requested by calling the IRS toll-free number, 1-800-829-3676. If you do not already have a United States Social Security Number for tax purposes, it is best that you apply for this number at your nearest Social Security office in the United States indicating that you wish to *file U.S. tax returns*. Otherwise, they may reject your application for a number. If you do not have this number at the time you file a United States tax return, the IRS will assign you a temporary Social Security Number.

Form 1040NR is relatively easy to complete, however, if you do not file your own Canadian return, you will likely need someone experienced in the Canada — U.S. tax treaty to assist you.

The Long Arm of the Law

Is there a statute of limitations for not reporting rental income for non-residents?

— *Wanda M., Kitchener, ON*

There is a statute of limitations of 3 years with the IRS if you have filed a completed Form 1040NR. If you have not filed or you filed without reporting all income, the statute of limitations does not apply, and the IRS can go back as far as they like to collect prior taxes. Prior to 1990, people in your situation had little to fear if the IRS ever caught up with them, because they typically made no net profit on their rental income. So, all you would need to do, is file a return for the years in question, and prove there was no net income.

However in 1990, the IRS came out with new regulations that do not allow non-resident filers the ability to file a new return deducting rental expenses against rental income longer than 16 months past the due date of the return. Consequently, beyond the 16 months allowed, tax on the gross rents, plus interest and penalties would apply irrespective of whether you made any net profits. To reconcile with the IRS, you need to first insure you file your 1991 tax return by June 15, 1992 (the deadline for the Form 1040NR). I would also recommend going back and filing for 1990 and the previous years, if you had rental income.

Regardless of whether you pay the withholding tax of 30%, or choose to file the Form 1040NR, you must still report the income earned to Revenue Canada on your annual T-1 return. You can take a foreign tax credit against the Canadian taxes due, for taxes paid in the U.S. Remember, filing a United States return and paying United States taxes does not exempt you from Revenue Canada reporting requirements.

Registration for Tax Purposes

Why doesn't the IRS require documents to be filed at the date of purchase that would register aliens with them for tax purposes?

— *Renu S., Windsor, ON*

The I.R.S. expects everyone to know the rules, and apparently has no sympathy for those who get caught for unintentionally not paying their taxes.

Residency for Tax Purposes

Do I need to have a "Green Card" or other visa before I am considered a U.S. resident for tax purposes? Are there other regulations that apply to becoming a resident for tax purposes without actually immigrating?

— *Oscar C., Sun City, AZ*

Residency for tax purposes does not relate to permanent resident status, but rather to your physical presence within the United States. The following is the general explanation offered by the IRS in its Publication 927, "Tax Obligations of Legalized Aliens." If you are in the United States as a lawful permanent resident (have a Green Card) at any time during the year, you are considered a resident alien for tax purposes and are taxed just like a U.S. citizen. That is, you are taxed on your income from any source throughout the world.

Even if you do not have a Green Card, you are still treated as a resident alien, if you are actually in the United States for enough days during the year. Generally, if you are in the United States for 183 days during that year, you are considered a resident for tax purposes for that year. But, you may also be considered a resident for a year, if you are in the U.S. for less than 183 days during that year, provided you were there for a certain minimum number of days, over a three year period. You do not count the days you were there under a diplomatic, student, or teacher visa. Since the United States and Canada have a newly ratified tax treaty, most Canadian visitors to the United States who stay less than the 183 days, would not be considered residents of the United States under the terms of the treaty. Consult a tax advisor if you are in doubt about your status.

Aliens and the 1040NR

My wife and I are Canadian citizens. In 1978, we bought a condo in Hallandale, Florida, which we have enjoyed in the winter for a three to four year month period each year. This year we sold our condo, realizing a small capital gain or loss. We have no other investments in the U.S.

In "Publication 519, U.S. Tax Guide for Aliens" (1989), which was provided to us by the IRS in Hallandale, one paragraph mentions that if "aliens have been in the U.S. for less than 183 days during a taxation year, gains from sales of capital assets are exempt from tax."

— *ISH, Hallandale, FL*

Your have done a good job in researching what your U.S. tax consequences are for selling your Florida condo. The "capital assets" that IRS Publication 519 refers to that are exempt from tax for non-U.S. residents are stocks, bonds and other such assets. Real estate and other real property are not included in this exemption for capital assets.

Consequently, your small capital gain on your condo may be subject to tax. However, before you calculate whether you have a gain or not you can add improvement and selling costs plus other related expenses to the cost basis or total amount you paid for the property. Regardless of whether you had a net gain or loss, you need to reconcile your sale with both the IRS and Revenue Canada. In the

U.S. you are required to file IRS Form 1040NR, the non-resident tax return for the year in which the property was sold, by June 15th the next year.

If the property was held in joint ownership with your spouse, you both will have to file, each reporting half of the gain (or loss). Since both you and your wife each are entitled to personal exemption of $2,300, your gain would have to exceed $4,600 before any tax would be due. If you did pay any tax to the IRS, you would receive a foreign tax credit on your Canadian return for the total tax paid. For Revenue Canada you will report the gain (or loss) on Schedule 3 of your T-1 tax form.

YOU STILL CAN'T
TAKE IT WITH YOU

NON-RESIDENT
ESTATE PLANNING

C anadians have not had to deal with any true inheritance or estate taxes since the Capital Gains tax was introduced in 1972. The provinces which had an inheritance tax at the time opted out of their own tax programs in favor of collecting the provincial portion of the Capital Gains tax from the deemed disposition at the death of a taxpayer. However, Canadian citizens (or Americans) owning property in Canada, need to become aware of the increasingly heavy hand of the tax man encroaching into their estates, when transferred to heirs, regardless of which country they permanently reside.

The first step in understanding cross-border estate planning is to understand all the forces of Canadian law that come into play, and the need for estate planning in the first place.

Many Canadians have become complacent and feel estate or inheritance taxes concern only Americans. However, on estates of less than $1,600,000 CDN, the Canadian inheritance or estate tax can be much greater than in the U.S. See Figure 8.11 in Chapter 8 for more details.

What, you say? There is no inheritance tax in Canada. Look again. The deemed disposition at death of capital assets with capital gains, and retirement programs such as RRSP's and RRIF's, create a substantial tax liability at death. In some cases, these hidden taxes have exceeded 53% of the value of the estate. Revenue Canada and the provinces do not call these taxes inheritance taxes but --- if it looks like a duck .....

The province of residence of the deceased, collects approximately half of this deemed disposition tax at death. Several provinces however, don't seem to be happy with their share of the tax, and are seriously looking at an additional death tax, coincidentally called what else but, an "inheritance tax."

Bob Rae, Ontario's NDP Premier, has been touting his "take from the rich and give to the poor" strategy, by bringing back an Ontario inheritance tax. He has engaged Neil Brooks, a socialist law professor, as vice-chairman of Ontario's Fair Tax Commission, to figure out ways to impose a "wealth tax" or a "death tax". With these kinds of people, and these kinds of philosophies in government, you can expect more of these taxes in the future.

British Columbia led the way by implementing a probate fee, with many other provinces following quickly behind. *The probate fee is a cleverly disguised inheritance tax, since the majority of one's assets go through probate either at their time of death, their spouse's death or both times, hitting the estate twice.* Family heirlooms can be taxed every time they are passed on to the next generation. As recently as June 1992, Ontario increased their probate fee by 300%. Alberta, in October 1993 raised its maximum probate fee by 600%. Because this so-called probate fee is an administrative type issue, it doesn't even need to come before provincial legislators for a proper debate, and the general public is kept in the dark until the fee is already in place.

Canadians or Americans who live in one country, and who own property in the other, face additional tax rules, which can leave them exposed to double tax. The double tax arises from the Canadian deemed disposition tax stacked on top of the United States resident/ non-resident estate tax, if applicable. This multiple death tax can total up to 80% of the property value in the other country. See the section titled *The Double Estate Tax* later in this chapter.

Canadians, particularly those who own property in both the U.S. and Canada, are setting their estates up for trouble in the form of high taxes, liquidity problems and high legal fees, if they ignore current inheritance taxes. Use the examples in Figure 4.1 to see what happened to the estates of some well-known people, as measured by estate shrinkage. Estate shrinkage, as the name implies, is simply the amount of the estate that was consumed by probate fees, legal fees, accounting fees, and estate taxes, before the beneficiaries actually inherit the estate.

From Figure 4.1, you can also see that there is a great deal of difference in estate shrinkage between these wealthy deceased persons. Why did Elvis Presley have a 73% shrinkage while Henry Kaiser, with a much larger estate, only 2%? *The answer is simple; proper estate planning techniques.*

Estate Shrinkage

Name	Gross Estate	Net Estate	% Shrinkage
John Rockefeller	$26,905,182	$9,780,194	64%
Elvis Presley	$10,165,434	$2,790,799	73%
Walt Disney	$23,004,851	$16,192,908	30%
Henry J. Kaiser, Jr.	$55,910,973	$54,879,958	2%

FIGURE 4.1

There are a number of planning techniques you can use to reduce or eliminate inheritance taxes -- regardless of your residency and whether you have property in both Canada and the U.S. This Chapter will provide you with some basic guidelines, and direct you to some of the most appropriate estate planning techniques for your situation. Remember that attempting to implement an estate plan without the assistance of a financial planning professional familiar with *both* U.S. and Canadian estate planning techniques, is analogous to reading up on removing your gall bladder, and then doing the procedure by yourself.

THE U.S. NON-RESIDENT ESTATE TAX

On November 11, 1988 President Reagan, in his last major formal announcement, signed the Technical and Miscellaneous Revenue Act (TAMRA) of 1988, making adjustments to the Tax Reform Act of 1986. There are two major provisions in TAMRA which affect Canadians who own U.S. property such as real estate, stocks, bonds or businesses. The first provision is a dramatic increase in estate or death taxes for non-residents on their U.S. property.

The second provision is the loss of the unlimited marital deduction by Canadians or non-U.S. citizens who are residents of the U.S. They can no longer transfer assets, estates or gifts tax free to a Canadian citizen spouse during their lifetime, or upon death. For gifts made after July 14, 1988, only the first $100,000 of gifts per year to a non-citizen spouse will not be taxed under this new provision. Prior to this revision in TAMRA, there were no tax disadvantages for Canadians who resided in the U.S. and who chose not to become U.S. citizens.

This dramatic increase in U.S. estate taxes -- which applies after November 11, 1988, affects Canadian and other foreign owners of U.S. real estate, company shares, debt securities and other property. Under this reform, estate tax rates on these investments jump from between 6% - 30%, up to 18% - 55% (depending on the taxable estate value).

Estate tax, can be analogous to income tax; there are two main factors which determine the amount of tax that is actually paid. These are, the tax rate in any given bracket, and the amount of the estate that it applies to. We will deal with each of these issues separately, and then combine them with some examples.

• The Taxable Estate

Estate tax in the United States, is technically a transfer tax on property owned at death. If the property is transferred during one's lifetime, it is subject to a gift tax at the same rates as the estate tax, with some minor exceptions noted in the section titled *What is a Gift Tax?* United States citizens and residents of the U.S. are subject to estate taxes on their worldwide assets, while non-resident Canadians are subject only to tax on their property deemed to be situated in the United States. The *Income Tax Rules* and *Estate Tax Rules* covered in Chapter 1 details what situations Canadians may be considered residents of the United States for estate tax purposes. *Estate tax is based on the fair market value (not just the appreciation) of all assets either on, or exactly nine months after the date of death.* The property subject to estate tax includes: real property located in the United States, personal property normally located in the United States such as autos, jewelry, boats, RV's, furniture and artwork, shares of U.S. corporations, regardless of where they were purchased, or where they are physically held, and certain bonds and notes issued by United States residents and corporations.

Assets normally excluded from the estate of an non-resident include: U.S. Bank deposits; government and corporate bonds issued after July 18, 1984; and shares or notes of non U.S. corporations. Chapter 6 provides more specific details, under *Exempt Investments* about which investments are exempt from both income tax and estate tax for non-residents.

The total of all taxable assets noted above, less any of the exempt assets and minus certain deductions for estate settlement costs and non-recourse mortgages, equals the taxable estate.

• U.S. Federal Estate Tax

Once the taxable estate has been totaled, the estate tax applies at the graduated rates, with the lowest rate being 18% and the highest 55% on estates over $3,000,000. Figure 4.2 shows the tax for some sample estates.

• Unified Credit

An estate tax credit of $13,000 for non-residents and non U.S. citizens is allowed to offset any estate tax payable. This effectively exempts the first $60,000 of the estate from taxation, as illustrated in Figure 4.2 and Figure 4.3.

Residents or citizens of the United States are subject to the same tax rates, but are allowed a unified estate tax credit of $192,800 which effectively equates to an exemption of $600,000.

U.S. Estate Tax

Taxable Estate	Tax (before credit)
$10,000	$1,800
$20,000	$3,800
$40,000	$8,200
$60,000	$13,000
$80,000	$18,200
$100,000	$23,800
$150,000	$38,800
$250,000	$70,800
$500,000	$155,800
$1,000,000	$345,800

(All figures in U.S. dollars.)

FIGURE 4.2

THE DOUBLE TAXATION ISSUE

Earlier in this chapter, we discussed the Canadian equivalent to estate tax, the deemed disposition tax on appreciated assets, including foreign assets at death. This tax is in effect, an income tax on capital gains. By its own definition, the United States estate tax is not an income tax. Consequently, Revenue Canada does not allow a foreign tax credit on estate taxes paid to the United States to offset the deemed disposition capital gains tax on foreign assets. In other words, there is no foreign income tax credit available from Revenue Canada since an estate tax cannot offset an income tax. Conversely, the American IRS, will not allow the capital gains tax paid to Revenue Canada as a credit or deduction against U.S. estate taxes payable, for exactly the same reason.

As a consequence, Canadians who own appreciated U.S real estate and other taxable U.S. assets, face two separate taxes on the same assets at the same time, without any real means of obtaining offsetting credit. This is double taxation.

Example: Non-Resident Estate Tax

Dorothy, a Canadian non-resident of the U.S., owns a villa in Hawaii her deceased husband had purchased for her over 15 years ago. The villa is valued at $300,000 fully furnished with a small mortgage of $50,000 remaining at a local bank. This property is all she owns in the U.S.

Dorothy's taxable estate is $250,000 (the $300,000 value of the villa less the $50,000 non-recourse mortgage).

Her estate tax from Figure 4.2 would be $70,800 less her unified credit of $13,000 for a net tax of $57,800 US

FIGURE 4.3

Figure 4.4 illustrates this double tax more clearly, by taking the example from Figure 4.3, and assuming that the owner of the Hawaiian villa were to die this year.

When the U.S. estate taxes are combined with Canada's death taxes, some Canadians could face aggregate taxes of more than 80% of the value of their highly appreciated U.S. investments.

The Canada — U.S. Tax Treaty does not cover estate taxes so Canadians are saddled with this discriminatory double taxation.

Prior to the new 1980 Canada — U.S. Tax Treaty, Canada and the United States did have an estate tax treaty. Negotiations are currently underway, and have been on going for nearly three years, to remedy this double jeopardy. To date, this issue has not been resolved, and it is not known if or when, a solution or a new treaty will be forthcoming.

This double exposure to taxation should spur Canadian investors to review their directly held U.S. assets, with a view to taking immediate action. There are Canadian tax rules that need to be

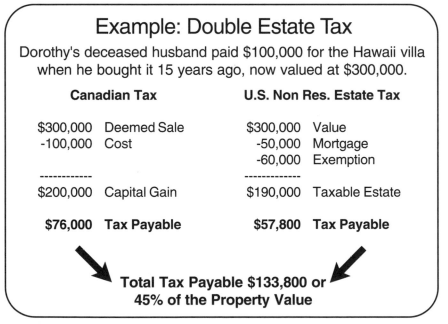

FIGURE 4.4

considered in any restructuring of U.S. investments, as well as on-going tax effects from transfers. Restructuring plans will have to be measured against the eventual estate tax savings to determine the merits of such planning.

There are a number of estate planning techniques designed to assist Canadians to avoid or reduce the effect of this non-resident estate tax. These techniques will be discussed in the next section of the chapter.

HOW TO AVOID THE U.S. NON-RESIDENT ESTATE TAX

Each of the following techniques have their individual merits and drawbacks in dealing with the non-resident estate tax. There is no silver bullet solution for all people in all situations. We will briefly attempt to state the circumstances in which each particular technique works best, and what to watch out for with each different option. Remember these options are given as a guide only, and any attempt to apply these methods to your own situation, should be accomplished with the assistance of a qualified cross-border estate planning professional.

• Become a U.S. Resident

In a previous section in this chapter, *The U.S. Non-Resident Estate Tax,* we mentioned the fact that residents of the United States receive an estate tax equivalent exemption of $600,000 compared to the non-resident exemption of $60,000. *A husband and wife who become United States residents would be eligible for a total exemption of $1,200,000 US or about $1,600,000 CDN, which is enough for many Canadians to be fully exempt from any estate taxes.* Without further estate planning, persons with larger estates could still be subject to tax.

There are many other implications of becoming a United States resident besides estate tax reduction. These ramifications will be covered in greater detail in Chapters 7 through 9.

• Mortgage Your U.S. Property

In the examples given in Figures 4.3 and 4.4, you will notice that non-recourse mortgages are a deduction from the taxable estate, and only the net equity is taxable. A non-recourse mortgage is from a lender whose only security is the property itself. In the case of a default, the lender cannot go after the borrower's other assets, if there is insufficient collateral in the property.

A side benefit of taking out a mortgage is that you may be able to deduct the mortgage interest on your Canadian tax return. If you invested the mortgage proceeds in the specialty type funds outlined in Chapter 6, *Exempt Investments*, you would be able to deduct the interest as interest paid to produce investment income. In addition, you could go a long way toward producing United States investment income which can protect you from a falling Canadian dollar.

We caution you to be aware of potential currency risks if you mortgage your property, and then take the proceeds back to Canada since your loan obligation is in U.S. funds. In this situation, a falling Canadian dollar would require larger Canadian dollar conversions with each payment.

Mortgages advanced through Canadian banks, or non arms-length lenders such as a controlled Canadian corporation, will not work for this strategy, since the debt would not be non-recourse.

• Joint Property Ownership with Children

Since each individual non-resident has a $60,000 estate tax exemption, it sometimes makes sense to place all family members on the title of an existing United States property, or when purchasing a new one. A family of five for example, could combine their exemptions and own a vacation home worth $300,000, and none of them would be subject to a non-resident estate tax.

On the surface, this strategy, appears very simple and basic, although it can be wrought with pitfalls.

Much as we may not care to admit it, our children are only human, and they will experience some of the not so pleasant things in life such as divorce and bankruptcy. Many an unsuspecting parent has had to pay off an ex-spouse, or a child's creditors, so they could keep their winter vacation home. In addition, family discord of any substantial proportion, can sometimes result in a battle over control of a family owned property.

If you have carefully considered these drawbacks and still feel this is a suitable technique for you, there are several things to consider concerning the actual placement of adult children's names on the property title. *If you already own this property, and want to place one or more children on title, there are both Canadian and United States tax implications of such a transaction.* First, Revenue Canada will consider this transfer subject to capital gains tax on the portion of the property being transferred. From a U.S. standpoint, the IRS will consider the transfer of the American property a gift subject to gift tax. A more detailed description of the gift tax appears later in this Chapter under the heading *What is Gift Tax.* (If both you and your spouse are not already on title, you can run into some of the same tax problems adding the spouse to the title.)

As a result, the best method to complete this type of a transfer is to sell a portion of the property to your children, even if you have to loan them the money in Canada at no interest. You can avoid the United States gift tax, but not the Canadian capital gains tax, if the property has appreciated. The capital gains tax, if any, could be paid by the recipient children, who likely are getting a pretty good deal anyway.

If you are about to purchase a U.S. property, this kind of arrangement is more easily completed at the time of purchase, rather than after the purchase is complete.

An additional benefit of this technique, is that the estate will likely avoid probate at the time of both parent's deaths.

• Have an Insurance Company Pay the Tax

Life insurance benefits from a non-resident insured person are not included in his or her taxable estate.

The recent development of no-load life insurance, has made this planning option more practical than ever. Most people who buy life insurance are unaware that an average of 150% of their first year's premiums, and 20% of the next nine year's premiums go for agent's commissions, manager overrides, marketing costs, sales trips to Hawaii and other related costs. *No-load life insurance strips out all these unnecessary costs so you enjoy both lower premiums, and cash values equal to your paid premiums, plus interest at fair market rates.* No-load life insurance works a lot like a term deposit, yielding slightly higher rates, but has the added benefit of a life insurance death benefit. It can be purchased only through some fee-only financial planners in the U.S. You pay a fee for their service, much as you would for hiring any professional, such as an accountant or an attorney. No commissioned agent should be involved. If you sell your property later, you can cash in your policy, and walk away with all the premiums, plus a good rate of return.

This method is simple, and can be very cost effective for most couples. Used in combination with the next method, *Establishing Appropriate Trusts*, it provides a worry-free, easy to maintain U.S. estate plan.

There are no negative tax or legal complications with this method, other than the interest earned on your policy must be reported to Revenue Canada, just the same as if you had earned the interest at a U.S. bank.

• Establishing Appropriate Trusts

In a manner very similar to the Canadian Spousal Trust, which allows the deemed disposition capital gains tax, ordinarily due at the death of the first spouse to be deferred until the second spouse's death, *there is the opportunity to defer United States estate tax until the death of the surviving spouse.*

The U.S. estate tax deferment is accomplished through the use of a Qualified Domestic Trust (QDT). This is a very simple trust created either during one's lifetime through a Living Trust with the QDT language, through a will, or by the executor of the estate. At the death of the first spouse, the QDT holds the decedent's share of the United States property in trust, under certain IRS guidelines, for the benefit of the surviving spouse for his or her lifetime. A further discussion of Living Trusts is included later in this chapter under the heading *Living Trusts -- The Simple Solution to the Problems of Wills.*

If the QDT is created under a Living Trust arrangement, you will achieve the added benefit of avoiding U.S. probate of your estate at either spouse's death, if you have the trust hold all your United States property. If you are transferring property into the Living Trust, you may face the deemed disposition tax by Revenue Canada, unless you ask for special consideration under the Canada — U.S. Tax Treaty.

This Living Trust/QDT, along with a joint and last survivorship no-load life insurance policy, is easily the best solution for most couples for coping with the non-resident estate tax. It is simple, flexible, economical, easy to maintain, and does not operate in any untested or controversial areas of tax law.

• Use Exempt U.S. Investments

Chapter 6 provides the details of U.S. investments you can use to generate income that is free from both U.S. income and estate tax. Use of these investments will go a long way toward simplifying your estate plan.

Unfortunately, real estate does not fall under the category of exempt investments, so it must be dealt with, under some of the other estate planning techniques. Remember, exempt investments, unless held in a Living Trust could be subject to probate in the United States.

• The Use of Canadian Holding Companies

Many Canadians hold U.S. winter homes or similar property by purchasing or transferring the property through a Single Purpose Canadian Holding Company. This is by far, the most complex strategy, and co-incidentally, the one most often recommended by lawyers and accountants on both sides of the border. *However, you should not be lured into complacency by it, or think that because of its complexity, it must work the best.* Of all the techniques described in this chapter, this method has by far, the most pitfalls and potential problems.

The logic behind the use of holding companies is that the holding company will never die, and if the company is Canadian, it will not be subject to U.S. transfer or estate taxes, upon the death of its shareholders.

This line of reasoning does have some merit. A holding company can work if you're buying land or a business for investment purposes, but those circumstances are extremely rare for most Canadian winter visitors, who normally purchase personal use property such as retirement or vacation homes.

One of the great pitfalls of having a foreign holding company owning personal use property is, it may not free shareholders from non-resident estate tax, which is generally the entire reason for forming the company. The reason is simple. The IRS bases what is subject to estate tax on incidents of ownership. Thus, it will pierce the veils of a corporation, or a trust, under these kinds of circumstances to determine who actually owns the property. This is particularly true if the corporate formalities have not been followed to a tee. Non-recognition rules, which are similar in both the U.S. and Canada, allow the IRS to technically reverse the transaction of placing the property in a foreign holding company, if it was created solely to avoid taxes, and there was no legitimate business purpose being served.

The second major pitfall deals with using foreign holding companies for personal use assets.

In a recent tax court case, the IRS ruled that individual shareholders living in corporation controlled property should have paid rent and had a formal rental contract with the company based on current market value rates. This ruling is in complete conflict with the rules Revenue Canada makes compulsory for the owners of a Single Purpose Canadian Holding Company. Revenue Canada states very clearly, that the property cannot be rented out, or any income earned by the company.

Generally speaking, if you set up and operate your holding company in the United States to meet IRS rules such as formally registering the company to do business in the state, filing state and federal tax returns, keeping corporate books and rental contracts with the owner shareholders, you will breach the Revenue Canada regulations and vice versa. This is an impossible legal situation to resolve.

The message is clear, the IRS never intended to allow the use of foreign holding companies to avoid non-resident estate tax by their shareholders, and will continue to attack them.

Even considering the pitfalls and the expense of setting up and maintaining a Single Purpose Canadian Holding Company, many advisors who are unfamiliar with other solutions to the estate tax, continue to advise their use. They justify their recommendations by saying *even though the holding company may not avoid estate tax, not using one means the property is certain to be taxed.* With all the other more economical and viable alternatives, why gamble your time and money on the one technique that is only a *maybe* method of avoiding estate tax?

We continue to recommend that Single Purpose Canadian Holding Companies be used under very limited circumstances. We believe their use does little more than generate unnecessary paperwork, raises your costs, and at best, are a long shot.

- **Sell Your Property and Rent**

Although it may seem a bit drastic to sell your property and rent each year, this can be a very good alternative for some people. It is a simple solution and the only tax consideration is possible capital gains tax on the sale of your property, to the IRS and Revenue Canada. With the steep decline in real estate values in many areas during the past few years, there may not be any problem with capital gains either.

The proceeds from the sale of the home should be invested in United States tax exempt investments, to generate U.S. dollar income to finance future winter stays.

If the death of the property owner is anticipated in a short period of time, a quick sale to a family member in Canada could be a very smart estate tax saving move.

IS YOUR CANADIAN WILL VALID IN THE UNITED STATES?

There are plenty of legitimate concerns among Canadians owning property in the United States about whether their Canadian wills will be valid in the United States at the time of their death.

Generally speaking, if your Canadian will has been drafted correctly, and is valid in Canada, it will also be valid in the United States. There is no real need to have separately drafted wills for American and Canadian property. There is however, some merit to having a separate United States will drafted in the state you normally reside in, to simplify the probate process. However, having two wills can also create problems, like trying to convince the courts which one is the correct one. In addition, you will have to pay for and keep track of two separate wills when it is usually unnecessary.

If you do not have a valid will in either country, your estate will be subject to the intestate laws in your place of residence. This creates double work for your appointed executor when there are assets in two separate jurisdictions such as a Canadian province and a U.S. state. *Many people ignore the need for a will, or do not look at alternate estate planning vehicles, because they are under one or more misconceptions about wills, joint ownership and the probate process.*

PROBATE comes from the Latin word meaning to "prove." After a person dies, probate is the process of proving how the deceased person wanted his or her property distributed. This "proof" is accomplished by presenting the will to court for probate.

Unfortunately, it isn't always that easy. You may know someone who has been through the frustration and the expense of probate. To help you better understand wills and the alternatives now available, here are twelve costly misconceptions:

• **Misconception #1.** Probate costs are small.

Wrong! Most personal representatives hire an attorney to help with the paperwork of probate. Here's why: The laws relating to probate and estate administration are extremely complex for a lay person. So while provincial and state law does allow a personal representative to go through the probate without a lawyer's help, most personal representatives do not want to face this challenge alone. So they hire a lawyer. Legal fees for even a simple probate, taking less than one year, can reach $5,000 to $10,000. Provincial probate fees can add 1.5% of the value of the probate estate to the total costs.

Total legal fees, and other estate administration costs can average from 3% to 10% of the total estate value, depending on the complexity of the probate. Owning property in both the United States and Canada definitely increases the complexity of the probate.

- **Misconception #2.** Your will and your assets remain private.

Sorry! Probate is a matter of public record, so all of your assets and liabilities will be spelled out to the penny in court records. Names of beneficiaries, and the amounts of their inheritance are all open to the public. Anyone can go to the court and ask to see your probate file. If you valued your privacy in life, you'd probably find probate uncomfortable.

- **Misconception #3.** A will can be probated in just a few weeks.

Even with a simple estate, probate can take from ten months to two years. During that time, the deceased person's property must be inventoried and appraised. Relatives and beneficiaries must be notified. Creditors must be notified and paid. Income taxes must be paid. Any contested claims and contested inheritances must be settled. Only then is the property distributed to the beneficiaries.

- **Misconception #4.** A will helps you avoid taxes.

No. A standard will does nothing to lower your taxes. A properly drafted will may take advantage of certain estate planning options such as setting up trusts that can save or defer estates taxes. A standard will simply indicates how you want your property distributed, and who you want to care for your children.

- **Misconception #5.** A will or a testamentary trust (a trust set up by your will) avoids probate.

All property governed by a will must go through the probate process by law, before it passes to beneficiaries. The law does not allow minor children to inherit bank accounts, stocks and bonds, or real estate. That is why parents often set up a testamentary trust for their children, which holds the property until the children reach the age of majority. But since the testamentary trust is part of the person's will, it still must be probated by the court.

- **Misconception #6.** Joint tenancy is the safest way to own property.

No. Joint tenancy with right of survivorship exposes each party to the debts of the other. For example, assume you own a home in joint tenancy with your child. Your child starts a business that goes broke. His creditors are chasing him trying to collect their money. The home you own with your child could now be taken away from you to satisfy your child's debts.

Also, joint tenancy property must go through probate when the second person dies, or in the event both people die in a common accident.

- **Misconception #7.** Your permanent home and your vacation home can be handled through the same probate.

Yes, but only if they are located in the same province or state. If you own a home or property in another province, or in the United States, you'll need to open a second probate, which means you'll hire another lawyer. This usually doubles the probate expense. And, if you own real estate in a third location, you'll need to open a third probate and hire a third lawyer.

- **Misconception #8.** A will prevents quarrels over assets.

Wrong! Wills are the subject of more lawsuits than any other document. Today, it is common for unhappy friends or relatives to contest a will, resulting in higher legal fees and added delays. This is one more reason why the average probate takes from ten months to two years.

- **Misconception #9.** Family members can sell property in the estate to raise money.

No. The court freezes the estate's assets until the probate has ended. The court may allow the personal representative to give family members small living allowances, but only up to the amounts allowed by provincial or state law. Permission to pay beneficiaries out of the estate must be granted by the court. Regardless of the outcome, asking the court's permission to sell property, increases the legal fees.

- **Misconception #10.** A will from one province is not legal in another or in the United States.

Not true. If the will is legal in one province, it is also legal in another, and in the United States. However, if your will contains certain legal language, it can go through probate more quickly and smoothly. If you want to avoid delays in probate, you might want to have your will reviewed by a lawyer in each province or state, in which you own property that must go through probate.

- **Misconception #11.** The cost of planning your estate is only the cost of drawing up your will.

No. The cost of any estate plan is both the cost of drawing up the documents, and the cost of carrying out the plan. If your will costs $150.00 in legal fees, and the probate costs $5,000.00, the cost of your estate plan is $5,150.00. This is a lot more than merely the cost of the will. This will is not only the most common document in our legal system, it is also one of the most expensive.

- **Misconception #12.** You must name your lawyer as your personal representative.

No. When you name your lawyer as your personal representative, you are in effect, giving him your permission to get paid twice. Once, for acting as your personal representative, and again when he acts as your lawyer. You can select anyone you wish to be your personal representative. For convenience sake, you may want to choose someone who lives in your province or state.

LIVING TRUSTS - A SIMPLE SOLUTION TO PROBLEMS WITH WILLS

A Living Trust is a legal entity that is formed to hold your property for your benefit while you are living. After an estate planning lawyer drafts your Living Trust, he helps transfer your assets into the trust. *Property held by a Living Trust does not go through probate after death.*

Here's why: The law says that any property owned when you die must go through probate, with a few exceptions such as joint tenancy property. When you set up a Living Trust, property is transferred into the trust and retitled in the name of the trust. So, after your death, the property doesn't have to go through probate, because the property is no longer in your name, it's owned by the trust.

If you want to manage the trust, name yourself as trust manager, or "trustee." A trust company's involvement is not needed at all. As trustee, you can (a) put property into or take it out of the trust, (b) change the trust, and even (c) revoke the trust -- anytime you wish. If you want someone to manage the trust for you, you can select a relative, friend, lawyer, bank, or trust company. Normally, both husband and wife are trustees while either are still living. In the case of death or disability, a successor trustee is named in the trust document, usually the same person who would be your personal representative in your will. While you are living, the operation of the trust provides you with all the same rights to your property, and your personal affairs operate pretty much the same as before.

When you form a Living Trust you accomplish the following:

• Save your family thousands of dollars in legal fees.

• Save your family months of lengthy court proceedings.

• Keep your family's legal affairs out of court records.

• Protect your family from the dangers of joint tenancy.

• Reduce the likelihood that your wishes will be challenged by unhappy friends and relatives.

• Give your family complete control over the property, because the trust assets are not frozen by the court.

• Avoid added probates for property you own in other provinces or states.

• Provide more efficient management of your estate in the event of death or disability.

As you can see, a Living Trust can be a very useful tool in cross-border financial planning, particularly when it has the Qualified Domestic Trust provisions, mentioned earlier in this chapter, for deferring non-resident estate taxes. Living Trusts are a very common estate planning vehicle in the United States, and are routinely recommended by estate planners at all levels. In fact, Canadians wintering in the United States see a continual barrage of advertisements for Living Trust seminars put on by banks, attorneys, brokerage firms and financial planners. Some use the Living Trust as a loss leader to sell other products or services.

A small number of Canadian lawyers and financial planners have begun to realize the benefits of Living Trusts. They should not be reserved for Americans only. Canadian trusts, like wills, are generally valid in the United States and vice versa. However, if you are going to use your trust to hold property in both Canada and the United States simultaneously, we highly recommend that you use a cross-border financial planner, to help coordinate legal services such as drafting the documents and the transfer of the assets, in both your home Canadian province and U.S. state.

POWER OF ATTORNEY - SHOULD YOU HAVE ONE?

One of the simplest and most useful documents you can add to your estate plan is Power of Attorney (POA). These will be of great assistance to you in almost all U.S. states and Canadian provinces.

These very basic documents give some other person(s), whom you trust, the right to transact business or make medical decisions on your behalf, if you are physically or mentally unable to do so for yourself. Anyone who has had a loved one in this situation may have discovered the long, costly and frustrating process of going to court to get authorization for a conservatorship or guardianship, so you can pay for this person's care. Correctly drafted, a Power of Attorney should eliminate the need for the conservatorship or guardianship.

To be effective, the POA must be a Durable Power of Attorney. A Durable POA means that it will be valid even after you become incapacitated, the point at which a non-durable POA would lapse.

Many lawyers in Canada and the U.S. recommend two separate Durable POAs, one for general financial needs, and one for medical needs. Good estate lawyers will routinely include the proper POAs with the wills and trusts they draft at no extra cost. Have the POAs reviewed by a lawyer in each of the jurisdictions that it is most likely to be used in, to insure they will be valid there.

Durable POAs are the kind of documents you hope you never have to use but when you need them, they are invaluable.

WHAT HAPPENS IF YOU DIE IN THE U.S.?

We've covered a lot of ground in this chapter on cross-border estate planning, but what actually happens when a death occurs? How does the IRS find out whether the deceased owned property in the United States?

Whether physical death occurs in either Canada or the United States, there is technically no difference with respect to taxes or any other obligations. At the time of death, either your personal representative or, if there is a Living Trust your successor trustee, has certain responsibilities. These are:

- Make a separate list of assets in both Canada and the United States and arrange for appraisals of the property.

- If the decedent did not have a Living Trust holding their assets, probates in the province(s) or state(s) where they owned property would have to be initiated.

- Determine what, if any estate tax is due to the IRS, and to the state(s) where the property is located.

- Arrange for the filing of the final tax returns in Canada and if necessary, in the U.S. by the appropriate deadlines.

- Arrange for the filing of the federal and state estate tax returns in the United States if the taxable estate, as defined earlier in this chapter, exceeds $60,000.

- If property in the United States is to be sold, obtain estate tax clearances for both the IRS and the appropriate state department of revenues.

- Hire and coordinate the professionals needed to execute all of these responsibilities.

- Notify beneficiaries as to their rights under the will or trust.

The IRS will normally learn about a death during one or more of the above procedures. *The Canadian executor, personal representative or successor trustee becomes personally liable for any estate tax due, if it is not paid correctly from the estate.* If there is no specified executor, the tax code states any person in receipt of a deceased person's property is considered to be that person's executor, known as a "Statutory Executor".

There is an automatic estate tax lien attached on all U.S. property of the deceased. These liens must be satisfied before they are released. If a personal representative wants to sell the property before the estate is finalized, he or she will be required to obtain federal estate tax clearance, and may face withholding taxes of up to 60%. The withholding tax may be refunded after the estate is settled by filing the appropriate returns.

Revenue Canada gives the personal representative six months from the date of death or to April 30, the year following the date of death which ever is sooner, to file the final Canadian return of the deceased, and pay any tax due. The IRS requires the non-resident estate tax return Form 706NA be filed within nine months from the date of death. Most of the United States including Arizona, California, Florida and Hawaii have their own estate tax, which is called a pick-up tax because they tax only to the extent that the IRS will allow a credit for state taxes paid. This does not increase the total amount of tax paid, but does mean that the IRS and the state involved share the equivalent of the federal estate tax.

Incidentally, estate tax returns are audited at least ten times more often than regular tax returns.

WHAT IS A GIFT TAX?

Throughout this chapter we have referred to gift taxes. This terminology is not familiar to most Canadians, but they hear it mentioned frequently in the United States. Gift taxes are paid by the giver not the recipient.

The U.S. gift tax is an off shoot of the U.S. estate tax. Gift tax is a transfer of property during one's lifetime, while estate tax is on transfer of property at one's death. The rates for gift taxes are identical to the estate tax rates provided in Figure 4.3 earlier in this chapter. Gift taxes have the same lifetime exemption as estate taxes, $60,000 for non-residents and $600,000 for U.S. residents and citizens. The lifetime exemption or any portion thereof, if used up through gifting, is not available for use as an estate tax exemption after death.

There is, in addition to the lifetime exemption, an annual gift tax exemption of $10,000 per donor, to each recipient he or she chooses. For example, a married couple with one child could give $10,000 each to the child gift tax free each year, and not reduce their lifetime estate/gift tax exemption. Non U.S. residents or non citizens, are allowed an annual tax free gift of $100,000 US in property to a non U.S. citizen spouse. U.S. citizens can gift unlimited amounts of cash or property to a spouse, anytime.

Canadians are subject to gift tax rules, whenever they give or transfer any U.S. located property. You should be careful and plan transfers of U.S. property accordingly. There are large penalties for failure to pay this tax, and ignorance of the gift tax rules will be of no help to you should you get caught.

CROSS-BORDER Q&A

Many of the issues covered in the preceding chapter of this book have been touched upon in the *Cross Border Q & A* column which appears in *The Sun Times of Canada,* and the author's own newsletter *The Sunbelt Canadian.* A majority of these questions have been posed by readers, looking for advice relating to their own specific problems or situations. At the end of this chapter, we have included some typical reader questions, along with our response, to better illustrate and flesh out the concepts presented in the chapter.

Does a Living Trust Satisfy Revenue Canada?

I have read your informative articles in the Sun Times of Canada, and the matter that most concerns me, is what will happen to my property, in terms of taxation when I die? According to information I have gathered from attending estate planning workshops, I could have a living trust. However, I need to know if this would satisfy Revenue Canada or the Ontario Government. These questions could not be answered by the American financial planners whom I have asked.

My house and property are located in Arizona, where I would like to live for eight months of the year instead of the usual six months less a day. How would I apply for resident Alien status? My efforts to reach U.S. Immigration by telephone have been thwarted by their computer answering system.

— *Morris P., Lake Havasu, Arizona*

You are correct in thinking that you should have a living trust as part of your estate plan. You can use this trust to hold both Canadian and U.S. assets. However, you need to be aware of some tax implications that Revenue Canada may catch you on. Revenue Canada considers most transfers into a living trust a deemed disposition. Consequently, if you have any potential capital gains in the property you are transferring into the trust, you will be subject to Canadian tax when you complete the transfer. If you are transferring your personal residence, or your gains are less than your $100,000 capital gain exemption, you will have no Canadian tax to pay. Items like term deposits, GIC's and bank accounts can be transferred in without tax consequences.

If your trust is set up correctly, it will allow your estate to avoid probate in both Canada and the U.S., which is generally a desirable goal for most people.

Since you are likely to be Trustee of your own trust, the trust will be a resident of the same country you are. This means that if you are earning income from assets in the trust, you will be subject to different sets of reporting requirements depending on the residency of you and the trust. For example, if you have Canadian bank term deposits in the trust and you are a resident of Canada, your trust will file Canadian tax returns to report the interest earned. If you passed this interest through to you personally, the trust would issue you a T-3 slip and you would ultimately pay the tax on your personal return. The trust would pay no tax by offsetting the interest earned on the term deposit with a deduction for the interest paid through to you, but it would still have to file its own return.

It is much simpler if you are a U.S. resident with a U.S. bank deposit. The Internal Revenue Service does not require the trust to report interest earned if you report it on your own personal tax return, cutting out any unnecessary duplicate reporting. Also, transfers of property into a living trust are not considered deemed dispositions and are allowed without tax consequences.

As far as your chances of immigrating to the U.S., you will likely need either a business or family sponsor to provide you with a realistic chance at a Green Card. There will be a Visa lottery the fall of 1992 and 1993 for U.S. Green Cards that Canadians will be able to participate in.

Where There's a Will There's a Way

I am a Canadian citizen, and I own property in Florida. May I legally bequeath this property or money to a relative who lives in Europe? If so, is a will appropriate or is there another way to accomplish this?

— Arial I., St. Petersburg, FL

You certainly may bequeath your Florida property to a relative in Europe. You can pass the property via your will, or by forming a simple trust. From the information you've provided, the only real advantage of the trust would be to avoid the expenses of probating your will in Florida. Keep in mind your executor or personal representative will have to file a U.S. Estate Tax IRS Form 706NA, and pay any U.S. non-resident estate tax if your U.S. property exceeds the $60,000 exemption. The tax, if any, would have to be paid before the property passes to your European beneficiary.

Changing Title & U.S. Tax Obligations on Florida Property

I am a Canadian, living seven months per year in Ontario and five months in Sarasota. Our house in Florida was jointly owned with my husband who passed away recently. How do I go about removing his name from any ownership documents? Also, I think my house would sell for $125,000 - $150,000. Please tell me the Florida laws that apply to Canadians.

— *Doreen A., Sarasota, FL*

Since you owned your Florida property jointly with right of survivorship, and are now the sole owner, you can simply have the title changed at your local county recorder's office. They will require a copy of your deceased husband's death certificate, and have you complete a basic form which varies from county to county.

You didn't say whether you had filed IRS Form 706NA and paid the U.S. non-resident estate taxes. This form needs to be filed within nine months of a death unless you received an extension, or your husband's U.S. assets were less than $60,000.

Form 706NA will detail how to calculate the non-resident estate tax due. You would be wise to get an appraisal of the Florida property, including the contents, as of the date of your husband's death. If the value of your deceased husband's share of the U.S. assets exceeds the non-resident estate tax exemption of $60,000, you will have to pay tax starting at 26% of the amount over $60,000. Although your filing will be quite simple, I recommend seeking professional help to complete Form 706NA, as it can be intimidating to do so on your own. Remember, if you have taxes due, interest and penalties for late filing will keep accruing, so you should get started as soon as possible.

Canadian Tax Obligations When Selling Florida Property

As a recent widow, I plan on selling my Florida home in the near future, preferably when the real estate market improves. I could use up-to-date information regarding the sale of real estate concerning Florida sales taxes and Canadian capital gains (or loss) taxes.

What is the advisability of changing the deed to joint ownership to a family member to avoid paying estate taxes. Is this change made through a Florida lawyer or my lawyer in Ontario?

— *Victoria S., Chatham, ON*

This question is quite similar to the previous one with respect to U.S. tax obligations, and filing requirements for a widow with Florida property. In addition to the U.S. obligations, you may have a Canadian tax to pay on the deemed disposition at your husband's death. The Canadian tax would be the capital gains tax on the appreciation of your Florida property on your deceased husband's share, since the time it was purchased. If your husband died before December 31, 1991, this tax would be due to Revenue Canada no later than April 30, 1992. The tax could be reduced or eliminated if your husband had not used all of his capital gains exemption in Canada prior to his death.

You need to be aware of the fact that changing the joint ownership with right of survivorship from your deceased spouse to another family member could cost you a hefty U.S. gift tax, if you do it all at once. If you are transferring U.S. property either while you are alive or via your will, you are subject to transfer tax in the form of a gift tax or estate tax, respectively. These taxes are levied at the same rates, with the gift tax having a $10,000 annual exclusion, and the estate tax a $60,000 once in a lifetime exemption for a non-resident. Consequently, a gift of $50,000 would attract tax on $40,000. The tax starts at 18% and must be paid by filing IRS Form 709NA.

You would be much better off selling a share of the residence to the family member and avoid this potential problem. If the family member has no money you can loan them the funds in Canada.

As always, we recommend you seek professional advice before you make any changes.

Computing Non-Resident Estate Taxes

My wife and I are joint owners of beach property, which we purchased in 1979. A special valuation was done and submitted to the IRS via Form 6661, prior to December 31, 1984, which covered the period from 1980 onwards. Can you elaborate on the non-resident estate tax, and whether it works on a sliding scale; assuming that the gross market value of the property was $100,000, $120,000, or $150,000, what would the applicable rate be for these three figures?

Finally, I have heard the terms "Community Property Agreement" & "Qualified Domestic Trust", applied to processes intended to reduce or avoid estate taxes in the United States. What do these processes mean and could they apply in our case?

— *James C., Redington Shores, FL*

The U.S. non-resident estate tax is applied to the Fair Market Value of a decedent's U.S. situs property on the date of death. U.S. situs property includes the decedent's share of jointly owned real estate, personal property normally present in the U.S., and U.S. stocks or similar investments.

A brief summary of the tax tables is as follows:

Taxable Estate		Tax Rate
$60,000	$80,000	26%
$80,000	$100,000	28%
$100,000	$150,000	30%
$150,000	$250,000	32%
$250,000	$500,000	34%
$500,000	$750,000	37%

You do not reach the 55% rate until the taxable estate exceeds $3,000,000. The first $60,000 of the estate is not taxed.

Since your property is located in Florida, and Florida is not what is classified as a community property state, community property rules give you no advantages. In Florida, it is important that each spouse contribute equally from separately owned funds, if you are going to put property in joint ownership with right of survivorship between spouses. If both spouses do not contribute equally to the

79

purchase of U.S. property, you can create other problems such as U.S. gift tax at the same rates as the above table, for the spouse who contributed the greater amount towards the purchase. Alternately, the IRS may consider the home to be owned by only the contributing spouse, for the purpose of calculating the non-resident estate tax.

A Qualified Domestic Trust can act as a mechanism to defer any non-resident estate taxes at the time of the first spouse's death. This can be a useful trust, and can be set up either before or immediately after the death of the first spouse. You are required to have a U.S. individual or corporate trustee, and will need to hire an estate attorney to draft the documents you require.

A Qualified Domestic Trust will not reduce the estate taxes but you can delay them in a manner similar to a Spousal Trust in Canada, with respect to capital gains tax at the first death of a spouse. There may be other, more viable alternatives to assist you to deal with non-resident estate taxes. However, this would require more information than contained in your letter.

Also watch for the results of the current Canada — U.S. Tax Treaty negotiations. These negotiations could possibly provide relief from this non-resident estate tax.

Single Purpose Canadian Holding Companies

This concerns a recent Sun Times column about Single Purpose Canadian Holding Companies. Two Ontario readers asked what to do with their existing Canadian holding companies that were formed to avoid U.S. non-resident estate taxes on their Florida properties. They discovered, to their dismay, that the holding companies would not likely do what they were established to do, which is avoid the non-resident estate taxes. Could you tell me why? Please provide more details.

— Billy A., Toronto, ON

Because of this and numerous other inquiries, it is obvious there is a need to revisit this issue and discuss it in greater detail.

The two Ontario readers both had Single Purpose Canadian Holding Companies, which owned their Florida properties. For this type of holding company, Revenue Canada states that the company must be used only for holding the real estate, not for rental or income properties. Since this type of holding company does not have a source of income, upkeep, taxes and other related expenses are paid personally by the shareholder. For a holding company to have some hope of escaping the U.S. non-resident estate tax; the company must charge Fair Market Value rent to the shareholder, and all taxes and expenses must be paid by the company itself. Appropriate United States federal and state tax returns must also be filed. From the contents of their letters, it appears that these two Ontario readers, were not fulfilling the United States requirements, and if they were, they would be in violation of the Revenue Canada's requirements for a Single Purpose Canadian Holding Company. Confronted with this conflict in laws, the best advice to these and other readers, is to unload their holding companies as soon as possible.

It is my experience that most Canadians who have holding companies for their United States vacation properties are in the same position and hence, this advice would be appropriate for all of them.

As one of the accountants who called me pointed out on the telephone, holding companies can have some useful purposes in estate planning for non-residents of the United States, but in isolated circumstances, and for non-personal use property. However, for the vast majority of Canadians who use their U.S. property for winter vacations, there are far better methods than holding companies to deal with the non-resident estate tax. In addition, holding companies are complex and costly to set up and maintain. Why get involved with something so expensive and complex that may not do the job, after all is said and done? Your heirs may be forced to litigate with the Internal Revenue Service to settle the issue. There are several less costly and/or simpler methods to avoid this tax.

One popular method is to create a living trust in the United States to hold the home. If the trust is drafted correctly, up to $60,000 may be exempted for each family member. The trust also helps avoid the costs and hassles of U.S. and Canadian probate.

Another option is to have an insurance company pay the tax, rather than paying it directly. This can be done through a low cost, no-load, joint and last survivor life insurance policy designed specifically for this purpose. Because it is a non-commission paying policy, the cash values, are approximately equal to, or greater than the amount paid in. As a result, if the property was sold or the estate tax eliminated, the policy would have a greater cash value than was paid in premiums.

There are several other methods Canadians can use to avoid the United States non-resident estate tax. Options range from becoming United States residents, to placing a mortgage on the United States property, or giving the property to children.

Regardless of which method is chosen, Canadian residents holding United States assets of any kind, should seek professional advice on how to handle these tax issues.

If, after weighing all the pitfalls and examining every alternative to setting up a holding company for your United States vacation home, I recommend you attempt to get an advance ruling from the Internal Revenue Service, and if a favorable ruling is granted, follow it to the letter.

CHAPTER FIVE

DOCTOR IN
THE HOUSE

GETTING THE MOST OUT OF
COUNTRY MEDICAL COVERAGE

One of the most perplexing questions confronting Canadians wintering, or taking up permanent residence in the United States, is medical insurance. With new initiatives from the Clinton administration and private insurers jockeying for improved market share, U.S. health care plans are a complex and constantly changing topic. We must also keep making adjustments for Canada's rapidly deteriorating out of province medicare system.

The last thing people need to worry about when they travel, is becoming ill, or suffering an accident. Unfortunately, sickness and accidents respect neither your travel itinerary, nor your socio-economic status. A medical emergency can happen anywhere, at anytime, and to anyone!

Any unforeseen expense is important to today's traveller, and you will want to be protected, no matter how great or small the potential loss. Even minor problems, such as the loss of luggage, can be a traumatic experience for many travellers, ruining their holiday or business trip. A catastrophic illness or an accident outside Canada, can turn a trip into a financial nightmare.

Provincial Health Insurance Plans
Outside Canada Hospital Benefits

- **British Columbia** (604)387-3166: $75/day as well as a small payment by the B.C. Medical Services Plan for services rendered in the emergency room prior to admission.

- **Alberta** (403)427-1432: $100/day.

- **Saskatchewan** (306)787-7101: $100/day, outpatient - $106/day, day surgery - $235/day.

- **Manitoba** (204)786-7101: 1-100 beds - $334/day; 101-500 beds - $426 day; 501 or more beds - $815 day; pays the greater of 75% or per diem only in the case of referrals.

- **Ontario** (416)482-1111: $400/day for "high level" care; $200/day for rehabilitation.

- **Quebec** (514)643-3445: $480/day (including surgery in a day hospital).

- **P.E.I.** (902)368-5858: $495/day regardless of bed capacity.

- **New Brunswick** (506)453-2161: $402/day; higher rate possible but requires prior approval.

- **Nova Scotia** (902)424-4450: $475/day for hospital bill 50% for ancillary charges such as x-ray and lab bills.

- **Newfoundland** (705)729-5971: $350/day maximum.

All Provinces Cover Medical
100% of Provincial Level

FIGURE 5.1

To make matters worse, provincial medicare programs are constantly being squeezed by rising costs and decreasing income. Even Saskatchewan, the pioneer of the Canadian medicare system, has introduced user fees to help defray costs. In 1991, Ontario's OHIP, sent the travel insurance industry reeling with a drastic cut in daily hospital and other benefits outside the province. Ontario's move threw several insurance carriers out of the travel insurance business, because they didn't like the increased underwriting risks. Several others jumped onto the bandwagon, hoping to make big profits by cashing in on the fact that travel insurance premiums virtually doubled overnight. We can expect more of the same from all provinces. Quebec's Regie, which was the last remaining province with adequate out of province coverage, has also cut back its coverage in a similar manner to OHIP. A table of current provincial out of Canada medical benefit coverages, is listed in Figure 5.1 along with phone numbers to call to for more recent updates and changes.

There are still travellers, who are unaware of the increased need for adequate travel insurance. While provincial health and hospital programs may provide adequate benefits at home, a Canadian who finds himself in trouble outside the country, may discover his provincial plan covers only a small portion of his medical expenses. As illustrated in Figure 5.1, provincial plans vary considerably with respect to the amounts paid outside Canada. British Columbia at $75.00 per day for a hospital bed, currently pays the least. This is but a small fraction of what hospitalization actually costs, especially in the United States, where medical expenses may easily exceed $2,000 per day. In most U.S. hospitals, $75.00 a day, would barely get you a parking spot. Canadians should be aware that in many parts of the world, physicians and hospitals do not follow the Canadian system of billing, where the daily room charge is all inclusive and covers most services and treatments. Many hospitals outside Canada charge a fee for room and board, and then charge for every procedure and band-aid they use. The Ontario Ministry of Health has published a survey of heath costs in the United States, and what portion of these costs would be covered by OHIP. Figure 5.2 displays the results of that survey.

Travellers may be sold token insurance plans, only to discover that the plan they purchased is inadequate or does not cover them, when they need hospital and medical treatment. Your bargain medical insurance may be instead, a simple trip cancellation or flight accident insurance policy only. Many of you have heard stories of Canadians who were forced to mortgage their property in order to pay for U.S. medical expenses. Figure 5.2 certainly provides some dramatic examples, with respect to patient costs, for someone treated in a U.S. hospital without adequate medicare supplements. The purchase of proper travel insurance not only reduces financial risk, but provides peace of mind as well!

Many people purchase travel protection as a supplement to their provincial medical plans, prior to heading south for the winter. The typical insurance plan has an expiration date of less than six months. If an individual covered by these plans wishes to stay longer than six months, they either go without coverage or have to return to Canada to trick their insurance carrier into giving them extended

Coverage of U.S. Health Costs by Ontario's Medicare

Aliment	Hospital Stay	Total Cost	Medicare Share	Patient Share
Heart Attack	28 days	$87,600	$16,000	$71,600
Fractures	9 days	$38,525	$4,800	$33,725
Gall Bladder	7 days	$17,825	$3,400	$14,425
Mild Stroke	2 days	$5,534	$825	$4,709

FIGURE 5.2

coverage. Premiums have become quite costly, and a typical married couple aged 65 can expect to pay between $2,500 to $5,000 for a six month policy. Numerous travel insurance plans are available through travel agencies, insurance companies, the CAA, and premium credit cards. The types of coverage and premiums can also vary widely. Most plans have benefit limits of $1,000,000 for covered medical expenses, although some plans have no dollar limitations on benefits. Terms may range from twenty-four hours to a maximum of one year. Premiums are based on the age of travellers, usually with categories for those over age 65, and those under age 65, and may also be dependent on the number of people in a party. Nearly all carriers require you to purchase your coverage before you leave Canada. See Appendix F for a listing of the names, addresses, and phone numbers of the major Canadian travel insurance providers.

The Canadian Life and Health Insurance Association publishes a very helpful brochure on health insurance for travellers, and what they should know before leaving Canada. This brochure can be received free of charge along with a complete list of insurers by calling 1-800-268-8099 toll free in Canada.

All policies are not alike, and you often need to work through a maze of costly options to ensure coverage for all major travel hazards. Here are some pointers to help you through that maze:

- In general, you get what you pay for. Buying the lowest premium, may get you inadequate coverage. However, just because a plan is expensive, doesn't mean it won't have any gaps in its coverage. Premium alone, should not be the sole criteria for purchasing travel insurance.

- Check with your credit card company since some gold or premium cards will provide limited medical travel coverage for travel stays between two weeks and sixty days. These are sometimes included in the annual credit card fee. We must caution you to check out this type of coverage carefully, since many plans are inadequate.

- Look for a policy that covers all expenses that your provincial plan does not pay, with no limitations on standard doctor's fees, or daily hospital expenses.

- Check the upper limit of the policy. Many policies have total benefit limitations as low as $25,000, so you'll have to pay any costs over that amount that your provincial plan doesn't cover. Even a brief emergency stay in a U.S. hospital can exceed this limit. The largest single claim paid recently by a travel insurance company has been about $300,000, for a heart by-pass operation. So as long as your upper coverage limit is around this amount, you should be okay.

- Review the "exclusions" clause of your policy very carefully until you fully understand it. *Many policies will exclude coverage for any prior medical condition, or pre-existing condition as insurance companies like to call them, that has been treated by a doctor within the past year, or some other specified time period.* If you had, for example, a bypass several years ago, and receive an annual check up from your doctor, any hospital stays that are even remotely related to your heart may not be covered.

- If you have a pre-existing medical condition, look for a policy that will at least provide you with emergency coverage for that illness. If you are uncertain how your pre-existing condition will be covered, pick up the telephone and call the home office underwriting department of the company in question. Their telephone number is normally listed on their brochure or policy. Or, check Appendix F in the back of this book. A five minute telephone call may save you thousands of dollars.

- Talk to friends and other travellers who have made a claim through the insurance carrier you are considering, to see whether they were treated fairly, and their claims paid on time.

- Don't expect miracles from insurance companies when submitting claims. Most companies will they pay only according to the letter of the policy and have highly structured claims systems in order to prevent fraud. Some companies pay only after the provincial plans have paid their portion of the claim. Only British Columbia, Ontario and Quebec allow insurers to bill them directly on your behalf. With payments from Ontario, and some other provinces running many months behind, payment from private carriers will as a consequence, also be slow. The better travel insurance carriers will pay your claims quickly, without waiting for provincial plans to pay up.

- Look for a few of the better travel insurance carriers who have set up claims paying offices, and negotiated payment schedules with hospitals in the more heavily populated winter visitor areas in the United States. This will often mean much quicker claims processing. Instead of you paying the hospital and waiting months for reimbursement, you pay nothing and the hospital gets paid directly from the carrier. This valuable service is worth asking for, when shopping for travel insurance.

- Some provinces have reduced the repatriation allowance for returning Canadians back to Canada for further medical treatment. It currently costs about $10,000 to fly a patient by jet, back to their home province from the Sunbelt. Check your policy to see whether you are covered for the portion of the costs that your provincial plan won't pick up.

- Look for a plan that has a toll free or collect emergency assistance telephone number manned by the insurance carrier themselves, and not by a third party. It can be very reassuring to have a 24 hour hotline that you can call, if you need assistance or wish to verify coverages. Often hospitals will call this line for you, and establish any necessary liaison between you and your insurance provider.

REMAINING IN THE U.S. OVER SIX MONTHS

There are currently no Canadian provinces that allow you to remain covered by provincial medicare plans after absences of longer than six months. This is a real dilemma for those who want to remain in the U.S. for an extra month or two. Most travel insurance policies will cover you up to a maximum of six months, and will only pay if the provincial plan pays. There are really only three options for someone in this situation:

- Do nothing and hope the province will not find out that you were out of the province longer than you should have been. In the past this option would have been much less of a gamble, but with hungry provincial medical administrators looking to cut costs, we do not recommend this strategy.

- Find an insurance carrier that will cover you when medicare may not cover you, and for longer than six months at a time. At the time of this writing, we know of only one company in Canada that offers such a policy. We did not want to mention company names in any portion of this book except in Appendix F, but this unique service offered by Nomad Travel Insurance warrants special mention. The company was founded by John Ingle in 1960, after his entire family experienced a major medical emergency driving back from a Florida holiday. They provide an insurance policy called Nomad Plan Two, that will cover Canadians outside of Canada, who are not covered by medicare, at the same rates as their regular travel plan. You can even purchase this coverage without having to return to Canada. There are some exclusions and limitations, as there would be with any policy. Plan Two will pay a maximum benefit of $50,000 medical and $50,000 hospital, and coverage can be bought for only one year at a time. Nomad is planning to introduce a variant of Plan Two this year, that will increase the maximum limits on coverage to $250,000.

- Become a resident of the United States if you are eligible (see Chapter 7), and enrol in an American health care plan. This will be discussed in the next section of this chapter under *Insurance For Canadians Moving to the United States.*

INSURANCE FOR CANADIANS MOVING TO THE UNITED STATES

There are a great many myths concerning Canadians finding effective and affordable medical insurance, when they take up permanent residence in the United States. We have prepared plans for Canadians, both winter visitors and permanent residents, for a good number of years and have successfully discredited most of these myths. We have been able to develop a variety of alternatives that insure Canadians receive the best of both the Canadian and United States medicare systems. By combining the two country's benefits, you can obtain the best protection, with increased flexibility.

Canadians who are over 65 years old and have resided in the United States for at least five years, or are United States citizens, are eligible for complete United States Medicare regardless of any pre-existing conditions. The cost is approximately $300 per month, or is basically free if you or your spouse have contributed the minimum amount to U.S. Social Security programs. See Chapter 9 for more information about qualifying for U.S. Social Security. There are also numerous private insurance carriers that provide Medicare supplements, to fill any gaps in U.S. Medicare coverage.

For those under the age of 65, there are a wide variety of health insurance options. Health insurance works much like car insurance in the United States. If you want zero deductible, with your insurance company paying for the slightest scratch, you will pay a substantially higher premium then someone with a $1,000 deductible. With health insurance in the United States, you can choose your coverage and your deductible. For example, a person age sixty can get a health policy with a $2,500 deductible and a $2,000,000 coverage limit from an A.M. Best rated "A" company for less than $100 per month.

If you are under 65, and have a pre-existing condition, expect to pay higher premiums and/or have some conditions excluded from coverage. When choosing a health insurance carrier in the United States, stick to A.M. Best rated company with an A or A+ rating, that has been providing health insurance for at least 10 years. Read over any policy and its sales literature very carefully.

President Clinton has introduced a new medicare system to be denated in congress over the next year and to be fully implemented by 1997. The object of the plan is to have all legal residents and citizens of the U.S. covered by medical insurance regardless of medical condition. The U.S. proposed medicare system appears to be a hybrid of the current Canadian and U.S. medical systems. The big debate is will the new system work, what will it cost, and who will pay for it. However the outcome is likely to be such that Canadians becoming residents of the U.S. will likely benefit by having better access to the U.S. medical system.

WHAT HAPPENS IF YOU GET SICK IN THE U.S.

Contrary to what you may have been lead to believe by the Canadian media, you will not be left to die in the streets because you do not have large buckets of cash with you when you arrive in the emergency room. It is the law in every state that you cannot be turned away from an emergency medical facility because of your ability, or lack thereof, to pay for your emergency treatment.

If you are using a travel insurance company with an emergency assistance line, your first call should be to them, as soon as possible after entering the hospital.

If you are unable to make the call, instruct someone else to do it for you. The travel insurance company can be invaluable in providing you with reassurance, finding medical specialists, or just getting you home in the shortest possible time.

If you don't have travel insurance, contact your provincial medicare office during business hours at the first possible moment. It won't be quite as easy as contacting a private insurance provider with a 24 hour hotline, but you should receive some valuable assistance nonetheless.

Be careful not to over do it with medical treatment that can be deferred until you return to Canada. Out of province medical insurance will likely not cover elective type procedures, so you could be doing it at your own expense. Once again, if you are not sure what is or isn't covered, call the emergency assistance line and confirm the treatments that will be covered.

If your condition has been stabilized and your doctors agree that you are well enough to travel, your insurance company and /or the provincial medicare services will make the necessary arrangements to have you flown back to Canada for follow up treatment. The insurance company will normally make return to Canada arrangements for loved ones, and your automobile, if necessary.

Generally, you are exempt from any adverse consequences from the IRS or U.S. Immigration, if your stay in the U.S. has to be extended beyond normal limits as a result of medical reasons.

TAKE THE MONEY
AND RUN

AN INVESTORS GUIDE
TO THE U.S.

The future outlook for the Canadian dollar is highly uncertain, and many experts are predicting a further decline from current levels. Few, in fact, are predicting any increase relative to the U.S. dollar, in the very near future. One reason is that Canada's $370 billion national debt represents nearly 44% of the gross domestic product as compared to 32.9% for the United States. If you were to add provincial debt (a large number of the U.S. States, by law, cannot run deficit budgets), Canada's total debt comes to over 70% -- a higher proportion than any major industrial country in the world, except Italy.

Canada has had to pay a premium to finance this debt, therefore it must keep interest rates relatively high to reduce inflation, and attract foreign investment to bolster the Canadian dollar. The results have been economically punitive as currency exchange rates tend to closely follow interest rates.

Like the U.S., Canada has reduced interest rates in hopes of stimulating the domestic economy, thereby driving down the Canadian dollar. It could decline even further, as Canadian policy makers look to make goods and services more competitive. The real truth of the matter is that nobody can really know which way the Canadian dollar is heading. At best, experts can predict general trends in the direction of the Canadian dollar. The Canadian dollar continues to suffer wide swings in relative value to the U.S. dollar in the nineties. Therefore, you may want to take another look at investment opportunities across the border.

THE INVESTMENT OPTIONS

Many Canadians, unfamiliar with the U.S. financial system, lack the confidence to invest across the border. They may opt for leaving available U.S. funds in U.S. currency savings accounts at their local Canadian bank, where they'll earn a meager 1% - 2% interest. You'll also be without the security of being insured by the Canadian Deposit Insurance Corporation (CDIC). Contrary to what some bank employee may have told you, no Canadian Bank or Trust Company offers CDIC insurance on any U.S. dollar account.

This chapter is intended to help Canadians who want to take advantage of U.S. investment opportunities, while minimizing or eliminating any adverse income tax and non-resident estate tax consequences of such investments. Chapter 2 discussed the need to protect yourself against a fluctuating Canadian dollar, and how to obtain the fairest rate of exchange. Now, we will focus directly on the major investment options in the United States, in consideration with income and estate tax implications for Canadians who reside there part-time. These tax consequences were previously discussed at great length in Chapters 3 and 4.

• Certificates of Deposit

Term deposits, or GICs as they are known in Canada, are called Certificates of Deposit (CDs) in the United States. CDs are issued by most U.S. banks, or by savings and loans (S&Ls) which are very similar to Canadian Trust Companies.

Interest on CDs is guaranteed, and rates currently range from 2% to 4%, depending on the term selected. CDs are insured in the U.S. by an agency of the U.S. government, the Federal Deposit

Insurance Corporation (FDIC), for up to $100,000 US per bank, and per account-holder. The FDIC is similar to the Canada Deposit Insurance Corporation (CDIC). However, the CDIC's insurance limit is $60,000 CDN.

By filing an Internal Revenue Service (IRS) Form W-8 (provided by the bank), Canadian non-residents who invest in CDs or other similar accounts, will be totally exempt from U.S. income and non-resident estate taxes.

Funds invested in CDs are not locked in, like most term deposits or GIC's in Canada, and are fairly liquid. However, if you withdraw principal before a CD matures, you may be penalized, and could lose one to six months interest earnings.

• Mutual Funds

Mutual funds are diversified portfolios of professionally managed investments of any variety or mix of stocks and bonds. Also known as Investment Funds, these funds are very similar in both Canada and the United States. However, the mutual fund investor in the U.S. has a much broader choice, with more than 2,500 funds currently available. That should be more than adequate to suit any investment objectives with any level of risk.

There are even some U.S. dollar mutual funds available through your Canadian broker/advisor, provided you do not mind paying higher commissions.

Many mutual funds in the U.S., have reduced commission levels from around 8% to 4% over the past five years, and many are available to the investor at no sales cost. These are known as no load funds. When investing in mutual funds, read the prospectus before you invest and be aware of all the fees payable at the time of purchase, upon withdrawal and on an annual on going basis. There is a great diversity in how individual funds charge their fees, so careful shopping can save you a great deal of money.

If you are considering investing in mutual funds in the U.S., you'll find that most mutual fund companies and fund representatives are unfamiliar with non-resident accounts, including the use of IRS Form W-8. The use of a qualified investment advisor or Certified

Financial Planner who is familiar with Canadian investment in the U.S., and who works on a fee basis rather than commission, is recommended.

Returns from mutual funds are not guaranteed, and will fluctuate accordingly, though many growth funds have averaged 12% to 18% on an annual basis over the last 10 years. These returns are a result of the type of fund managed, and the skill of the investment manager.

Interest from U.S. mutual funds, and dividend distributions earned by non-resident investors is subject to a 15% U.S. withholding tax which can be taken as a full tax credit on your Canadian tax return. Mutual fund investments in the U.S.-- whether purchased in Canada or the U.S.--- are also subject to non-resident estate tax on amounts, over $60,000 US including all other U.S. property.

• **Money Market Funds**

Money Market funds are offered by both banks and mutual fund companies. When purchased through a U.S. bank or a savings and loan, these accounts are merely daily interest savings/chequing accounts. They are currently paying 2% to 3% interest, and are insured by the FDIC.

Money market mutual funds generally yield % to 1% higher than bank money market accounts, but hold various types of short-term government and corporate securities directly. There is no FDIC insurance on money market mutual funds, but if you select a portfolio of strictly U.S. government securities, you have the same government guarantee without the FDIC's $100,000 limit.

Money market mutual funds are fully liquid, and impose no sales charges to get in or out of a fund. Many also provide free cheque writing services.

• **Limited Partnerships**

U.S. Limited Partnerships (LPs) are similar to Canadian LPs. They offer an opportunity to participate directly, with limited liability, in various businesses and investments, while providing professional management.

A non-resident investing in American LPs, will be required to file a U.S. non-resident tax return, whether or not any taxes are due. Taxes paid in the U.S. will provide Canadian taxpayers a corresponding credit on their Canadian tax return.

Rates of return and safety factors for the LP investor will vary as greatly as the myriad of types of LPs available. Great caution is advised when choosing an LP, and professional advice from a qualified investment advisor or Certified Financial Planner is highly recommended.

LPs are considered long-term investments and generally require you to commit your investment until the LP matures, normally 5 to 7 years or beyond. They are more suited to resident investors, but a large number of them will accept non-residents. The fair-market value of an LP is subject to non-resident estate tax on estates in excess of $60,000 unless the underlying securities in the LP are exempt investments.

• Real Estate

Real estate investments in Canada and the U.S. are dependent on the same three principals: location, location, location! Investors must do their homework in order to be successful.

Canadians choosing to invest in the U.S. will find much more paperwork than they may be accustomed to, and some unfamiliar terminology.

For instance, rather than using an attorney to complete the paperwork, most U.S. investors are required to use the services of a title insurance company. These companies complete the necessary paperwork and provide trust services for the equitable exchange of funds between buyer and seller. They also provide the mandatory title insurance required to ensure there is clear title to the property. The buyer typically pays for this insurance, which can range from $500 to $1,000 or more on an average residence.

Much like marriage has far less paperwork than divorce, real estate purchases are much easier to complete than sales. When a non-resident sells, or is deemed to have sold property in the U.S., they are required to file a non-resident U.S. income tax return, reconciling any capital gains or losses in the year of sale. Without proper clearance certificates from the IRS, the non-resident may be subject to federal and state withholding taxes.

If you are placing a mortgage on your property, you should find an institution familiar with the unique requirements of U.S. non-residents. You will likely be confronted with additional mortgage costs known as "points or closing fees." Points and closing fees are the institution's way of covering the up-front costs of handling the mortgage, and may reduce or discount your mortgage interest rate.

The value of your equity in any real estate, together with your other U.S. assets, is subject to estate taxes over the $60,000 exemption on property held by non-residents.

• Specialty Funds

A handful of mutual fund families have recently created a variety of investments aimed specifically at the non-resident U.S. investor. With these funds, which are registered outside the U.S., Canadian investors can enjoy the advantages of U.S. dollar investments and investment advice while avoiding any adverse tax consequences. *They are fully exempt from any United States income or estate tax, plus there is no need for IRS Form W-8 and no income tax reporting requirement to the IRS.*

Because these funds are managed in the same way as standard mutual funds, they give you access to professionally managed portfolios corresponding to various asset classes. For example, there are funds specializing U.S. government bonds, or Japanese stocks, Canadian stocks, German government bonds, and so on. The mix of funds you choose will depend on your investment objectives. Once you have opened an account with these funds, deposits and withdrawals can be made easily, and periodic dividend cheques can be mailed to you anywhere, or deposited in your local bank account.

Specialty funds are only available to non-residents and/or non-citizens of the U.S., and cannot be purchased while you are in the United States. If you want to maintain their exempt status, you must open your account while outside the United States. Purchases must be directed through U.S. stockbrokers. Commissions can be substantial, with front-end sales loads as high as 5%, and redemption fees of up to 4%. Many of these funds sport high annual expense ratios of up to 3%! Selling brokers are compensated from one or more of these expense categories. We are not aware of any true no-load specialty funds at this point.

- **Specialty Portfolios**

Specialty portfolios are professionally managed portfolios solely comprised of the exempt investments listed below, and tailored to each investor's personal objectives and preferences. Investors with $100,000 US to invest, who want international diversification, quick access to funds, and managers who work on a fee basis rather than commissions, should consider this alternative. These portfolios are managed only for non-residents. Only a limited number of investment firms manage specialty portfolios. Finding the right firm may be time consuming, but the increased flexibility, safety, and cost savings can be well worth the effort. Refer to the end of this chapter for details on how to locate a specialty portfolio manager.

EXEMPT INVESTMENTS

Throughout this book, we have periodically referred to exempt investments, meaning U.S. investments that are exempt from both income and estate tax for non-resident. You should already be familiar with the fact that exposure to U.S. taxes can be a direct function of the type of investment you make in the United States.

The list of the exempt investments detailed below can be your guide to eliminate those investments that can create unnecessary tax burdens for the non-resident, while at the same time allowing them a number of choices to develop a safe, income producing portfolio of U.S. investments. Exempt investments include:

- Banking and Savings & Loan deposits, including CDs, savings accounts, and money market funds. A completed Form W-8 must be filed with the savings institution.

- U.S. Treasury bonds, notes, bills, and agency issues if issued after July 18th, 1984.

- U.S. Corporate bonds, if issued after July 18th, 1984. A completed Form W-8 must be filed with the company issuing the bond or the brokerage account where you purchased and hold the bond.

- Specially structured mutual funds. These are the specialty funds explained in detail in the previous section of this chapter titled *Specialty Funds*.

- Some investment companies or brokerage houses offer money market funds where the securities in the portfolio consists of only government and corporate bonds that have been noted above as exempt securities. A completed Form W-8 must be filed with the brokerage firm.

- Life insurance death benefits regardless of the amount.

UNDERSTANDING INVESTMENT RISK

Most investors think of risk in two erroneous ways. The first is that investment risk reflects only potential downward movement in the value of an investment. In reality, risk is a measure of market volatility. Therefore risk reflects both the probability of upward and downward price fluctuations.

The second assumption is that "market" risk is the only kind of risk that exists in today's investment marketplace. Market risk is the degree to which an investment's price behavior correlates with the general market for that investment. A good example of this is stock, whose value will generally reflect upward or downward movements in the stock market as a whole.

This section will outline at least seven types of investment risk, and place special emphasis on those types of risk, which can most effect retirees or persons planning for their retirement.

- **Specific Risk** reflects risks inherent to one investment in particular. A purchaser of GM stock would be concerned about problems peculiar to GM, such as the amount of debt, potential labor problems, effective management, and so on. This type of risk may be eliminated by properly diversifying a portfolio.

- **Market Risk** is best exemplified by the stock or real estate markets. Market values of individual stocks or parcels of real estate tend to follow movement in the stock market or regional real estate markets in general. Market risk can pose a substantial short-term risk to investment principal. If your investment horizon is greater than three years, market risk in the stock market decreases rapidly, and continues to decrease the longer the time period of your investment.

- **Inflation Risk** is the most insidious and harmful risk to retirees, largely because its effects are not immediately obvious. Inflation reflects a loss of purchasing power, and it primarily effects fixed investments such as bonds, term deposits, GICs, CDs, and annuities. If an investor had $10,000 in Canada Savings Bonds which yielded 10% per year in income, and inflation averaged 5% that year, what happens to the value of the bonds? The bonds will still be worth $10,000 on the investor's annual statements, but will the investor still be able to purchase $10,000 worth of goods and services? The answer is no. Because of the 5% annual inflation, the investors $10,000 is worth 5% less, or $9,500! Income from the bonds is also worth 5% less, compounded for each year of inflation! If the investor held these bonds for ten years, and inflation averaged 5% per year, the investor would get a check from the Canadian government for $10,000, but the bonds would purchase only $6,139 worth of goods and services. This type of risk may be reduced by adding inflation hedges to a portfolio.

- **Interest Rate Risk** reflects how movements in interest rates effect the value of investments. Anyone whose income depends primarily on interest rates has seen their income effectively cut in half from 1991 to 1992 as their term deposits come due for renewal. Interest rate volatility over the last 15 years have made bonds and term deposits much more risky to hold, particularly in a portfolio that has little or no diversification.

- **Currency Risk** is similar to inflation risk in the way that it affects investments. This type of risk is especially important to Canadian retirees and was exemplified in Chapter 2. Changes in the value of currencies can affect purchasing power the same way inflation does. For instance, if the Canadian dollar were to depreciate 5% in a year relative to the American dollar, Canadians could purchase 5% less in American goods. Over $200 billion of currency is traded each day all over the world, up from almost nothing in the 1970's. This type of risk may be eliminated by diversifying a portfolio in the global sense.

- **Economic Risk** affects investments much like market risk. Stocks and real estate tend to do well when the economy is brisk. Gold and utilities are examples of "counter cyclical" investments, which perform well when the economy is down.

- **Government Risk** affects both Canadian and American residents. This type of risk results from both government's frequent changes to the tax laws — often with negative effects for the investor. The most recent example was the Tax Reform Act of 1986, in the United States, where many tax shelter investors lost their tax preferences, and were not grandfathered from the effects of the new law. Real estate is still struggling to recover from this change after seven years. This type of risk may also be reduced by properly diversifying your portfolio.

By knowing all of the risks inherent to investing, and prudently diversifying investments, the informed investor can enjoy a high, tax-favored income at low levels of risk. The effects of inflation and wide currency swings can be minimized.

THE REWARDS OF GLOBAL INVESTING

In 1990, Merton Miller, William Sharpe and Harry Markowitz won the Nobel prize in economics for their pioneering work in quantifying returns and risk from a portfolio perspective. Their research turned up some rather surprising results. It turns out your grandmother was right after all; don't put all of your eggs in one basket. The market may not compensate you for the additional risk with higher returns. There is also no such thing as a free lunch. Decrease your overall risk, you will also decrease returns over the long run.

Most surprising, were the results attained by combining two assets that behave differently. Take a stock that performs well during economic downturns, and take a cyclical stock. Both are expected to return 11% over the long run. If you buy equal portions of both stocks, the long-run return will be 11%. But year to year volatility will decrease, because one stock does well when the other does poorly. In fact, adding an asset that may be risky, may actually reduce the total risk of the overall portfolio!

What does this have to do with international investing? International stock and bond markets do not move in lockstep with the U.S. and Canadian stock markets. For example, many European markets, as well as the Japanese market did poorly in 1991, while North and Central American markets skyrocketed. By combining foreign stocks and bonds with U.S. and Canadian investments, we should lower risk and enhance returns over the long run.

Invest in foreign securities and you attain diversification through exposure to different economies. Over the last 20 years, many markets have grown faster than the U.S. or Canadian stock markets. This means added profits for investors. Investment opportunities may also emerge with the opening of eastern European countries and former republics of the Soviet Union.

Currency risks are also hedged. Canadian investors in foreign securities would have benefited greatly from currency gains when the Canadian dollar dropped from $0.89 US to $0.83 US in less than six months from late 1991 to early 1992. Since we are becoming a global economy, diversifying currency risk is very important.

More aggressive investors may find excellent opportunities in "emerging markets". Some of these markets have boomed during the last few years. Many Latin American countries have freed up their economies with skyrocketing stock markets as a result. Mexico, Chile, Argentina, and Brazil are recent examples. Indian and Hong Kong markets are also exploding. While we don't recommend that a portfolio contain only emerging market stocks, an exposure of 10% or so may aid returns and lower portfolio risk.

How do you select and purchase shares of stock or bonds in these markets? By using a mutual fund, stock selection is left to experts who focus on the country in question. This expertise can be crucial since financial disclosure and accounting standards are rarely as investor-oriented as they are in the U.S. and Canada. Information on foreign companies is also difficult to come by. Since funds buy large blocks of stocks or bonds, transaction costs are reduced. Funds do all the paperwork and accounting. Shares can be bought and sold quickly and inexpensively, and offer instant diversification.

With U.S. and Canadian stocks markets looking more over-valued every day, and lower interest rates on bank deposits and government bonds, now would seem an ideal time to consider the diversification benefits and higher potential returns of foreign stocks and bonds. As always, we recommend you seek professional advice before implementing any of these ideas.

CHOOSING AN INTERNATIONAL INVESTMENT MANAGER

The key to successful investing is formulating a long-term, internationally diversified portfolio policy based on your own objectives and preferences. The first words out of a potential investment manager's mouth should be questions related to your personal investment objectives. These objectives should contain concise information regarding the returns you expect, and the level of risk or volatility you are willing to undertake in exchange for these returns.

It is also important to consider present and future income needs from the portfolio, investment time horizon, liquidity requirements, income and estate tax information, and your current estate plan. You should be active in these early stages when portfolio policy is being formulated, and again when your individual situation changes. Charles D. Ellis' book *Investment Policy,* 2nd edition, published in 1993, by Business One Irwin, is considered a classic in this area.

Unfortunately, in the real world, most advisors may be little more than sales people enjoying up-front commissions based solely on sales volume. Clearly, there is little or no incentive for an advisor to monitor a client account after a commission is received.

Moreover, advisors working on a commission basis, earn more by selling or shifting existing investments. This latter procedure, if done excessively, is called "churning" and is illegal.

The key to successful investment performance is active, professional portfolio management; with the most important considerations being the manager's investment philosophy, and the client's comfort with that philosophy.

Why is formulation of a long-term portfolio policy emphasized here? Because some recent studies from the Financial Analysts Journal (Gary Brinson, L. Randolph Hood and Gilbert L. Beebower, "Determinants of Portfolio Performance", July-August 1986, and Gary P. Brinson, Brian D. Singer and Gilbert L. Beebower, "Revisiting Determinants of Portfolio Performance: An Update", May-June 1991) show that more than 90% of investment returns generated by large pension plans are due to establishing and following a long-term investment policy. Less than 10% of portfolio returns were attributed to security selection "stock picking," or market timing (switching funds between investments or asset classes in response to perceived changes in the economy). The successful investment advisor will pay close attention to those decisions that will generate 90% of their portfolios' return.

There seems to be an inherently unfair bias in the way the investment marketplace treats "retail", or individual investors versus "wholesale" or institutional investors. What are these differences, and how can investors overcome them? How can you ensure equal treatment?

First, let's examine some of the differences. The retail marketplace is largely transaction-based. Stockbrokers, commissioned financial planners, and insurance salespeople are compensated by the number of financial transactions they effect. Put another way, the more they sell you, the more they make. The focus is not always on managing an investor's funds for the long-term, but on switching from investment to investment.

Even banks collect commissions indirectly. Term deposits or bank CDs, return an interest rate plus a guarantee of principal for a specified period of time. The banks invest the funds in government and corporate debt securities, mortgages, and leases, and other investments. The return is often significantly higher than what is paid out to bank depositors.

The institutional marketplace, which includes pension funds, insurance companies, and mutual funds, is performance based. Portfolios are often managed by one or more managers, whose compensation is based on how big the portfolio gets. They are paid for performance rather than buying or selling investments. Here, the incentive is to reduce commission costs, since commissions reduce the size of the portfolio they manage.

Individual investors are constantly bombarded by the media and salespeople with information about the latest investment guru, the hottest stocks, or the best market pundit. They often buy under the premise that the broker, salesperson, or financial planner can pick "hot stocks" or other investments (why is life insurance so often the hot investment?) and can time favorable moments to switch between stocks, bond or cash, depending on market conditions. If market timing and security selection contribute less than 10% of a typical portfolio's return, why does the media and retail investment marketplace focus so much time and energy promoting these advisors who claim to have exceptional abilities in these areas? Because strategies that lean heavily on security selection and market timing generate many, many more transactions (read: commissions) than establishing and sticking to a long-term investment policy.

Although many institutional investors use stock-picking and some form of market timing, an increasing number of them have become asset allocators. This involves the diversification of investments between cash equivalents, stocks, bonds, real estate, and other asset classes. Asset allocators do not try to predict the direction of the markets, the economy, or interest rates, since they believe these markets and indicators are unpredictable over the long run. They also diversify their holdings, and use a buy-and-hold strategy to minimize transaction costs.

How can you level the playing field? Find an investment advisor who focuses on formulating a long-term investment policy based on your needs and preferences, which is 90% of the ballgame. In choosing an investment manager, you should consider the following:

- Choose a manager compensated on the basis of performance, not commissions.

- All other things being equal, choose the manager with lower management fees.

- Make sure the manager cannot make "big bets" with your portfolio. Choose a fund or firm whose management philosophy requires the manager to be diversified to some degree.

- Choose a manager who uses no-load mutual funds and/or a discount brokerage arrangement to transact securities trades, thus minimizing your investment costs.

CROSS-BORDER Q&A

Many of the issues covered in the preceding chapter of this book have already been touched upon in the *Cross Border Q & A* column, which appears in *The Sun Times of Canada,* and the author's own newsletter *The Sunbelt Canadian.* A majority of these questions have been posed by readers, looking for advice relating to their own specific problems or situations. At the end of some chapters, we have included some typical reader questions, along with our response, to better illustrate and flesh out the concepts presented in the chapter.

Does U.S. Law Forbid Non-Resident Brokerage Accounts?

I have searched in vain, for a way out of my dilemma; the Florida broker I had dealt with for about a year was forced to close my account. Apparently regulations prohibit a non U.S. resident brokerage account, with or without a W-8, no matter which address I use. As a Canadian Snowbird and a former stock broker, I am familiar with all of the information in your recent article "Relax While Your Money Works." Please explain how I can resolve this.

— *Edouard S., North York, ON*

Your dilemma can be solved by calling Charles Schwab -- the United States' largest discount brokerage firm. Charles Schwab has what is called a NRA account (NRA stands for Non-Resident Alien) that you may use without restrictions. There is a little more paperwork involved to set up this account than an ordinary brokerage account, but it gives you full access to trade in your account, as you require. If you want more information about Charles Schwab, they have offices in major cities throughout Florida, and the U.S., and are listed in your local phone book. You may have luck with other brokerage firms for these NRA accounts as well.

I believe your stock broker was confusing his company's policy and procedures with that of the regulatory bodies, as there are no laws that I am aware of, prohibiting non-resident accounts if they are done properly.

Holding Securities in Street Form & U.S. Treasury Notes

If I hold U.S. securities in street form, in my Canadian account, are they still subject to the $60,000 limit for estate tax? Technically, the answer is probably yes, but are there reporting procedures between the two countries? Finally, I have read about U.S. Treasury notes. Are these available to Canadians? If so, where and how?

— Ron Z., Corunna, ON

Holding securities in street form, as you already guessed, does not exempt them from non-resident estate tax. Any United States securities, unless they are specifically exempt, add to the taxable estate of non-residents. Tax exempt securities that would likely be purchased through a brokerage firm include Certificates of Deposit from United States banks, U.S. Government Treasury Bills, Treasury Notes and Treasury Bonds issued after July 1984. U.S. Securities are taxable for non-resident estate tax purposes, whether the securities are held in Canada, the U.S. or anywhere in the world.

There are no automatic formal reporting procedures between Canada and the United States with respect to brokerage accounts. However, the Canada — United States Tax Treaty allows for the exchange of tax information in either country at any time. The Internal Revenue Service has been using this treaty clause quite frequently to catch United States taxpayers for not reporting taxes due. The answer to your final question about purchasing U.S.

Treasury notes is that you can hold as many as you desire, and if you open the NRA account with Charles Schwab, or another broker, you can purchase them there at a very reasonable cost.

Specialty Funds for Non-Residents

I am semi-retired, and like to devote time to my business and leisure. I spend 5 months of each year in the U.S., so I need U.S. dollar income. I am afraid that the Canadian dollar will continue to decline in value against the U.S. dollar. Are there investment advisors in the U.S. who manage accounts specially for non-residents?

— *Tom C., Phoenix, AZ*

A number of U.S. based mutual fund companies have started specialty mutual funds for non-residents. These funds are registered offshore in places like the Cayman Islands or Guernscy. They may only be purchased by non-residents of the U.S. while outside the U.S. and only through a U.S. broker. All of the funds we have examined are load funds, and exact their pound of flesh through one or more of the following ways:

- up front commissions,

- commissions incurred when fund shares are sold, and

- high annual costs, some of which are passed through to brokers.

To date, we have not encountered any no-load specialty funds that are available to the general pubic. Although somewhat expensive, specialty funds can be useful to investors with $100,000 or less, who understand that diversification is important to the realization of their financial objectives.

Another alternative is to choose an investment advisor who can manage a diversified, international portfolio specifically tailored to each investor's needs and preferences. This type of professionally managed portfolio generally requires $100,000 or more to be invested. These accounts can be specifically tailored for each individual, but should invest only in exempt investments, such as U.S. Treasury securities and corporate bonds issued after July 18, 1993, bank certificates of deposit, exempt money market funds, and specialty mutual funds. Accordingly, specialty portfolios should be exempt from U.S. income tax reporting and withholding, and not included in the non-resident's U.S. estate. Funds should only be invested in marketable assets that can be turned into cash within a week or two.

Specialty portfolios are appropriate for investors who desire:

• A custom tailored, long-term investment policy.

• Personal, one-on-one attention.

• Prudent, professional management of their investments.

• Privacy.

• Increased safety and returns of international diversification.

• Quick access to funds.

• Minimal commissions.

• Exemption from U.S. income tax reporting.

• Exemption from U.S. income tax withholding.

• Exemption from the U.S. non-resident estate tax.

Investors typically pay management fees of 0.5% to 1.5% per year, depending on the manager and the size of the account.

In 1993, Keats, Connelly and Associates, Inc., (KCA) launched a specialty portfolio management program called the International Managed account for Non-resident Aliens (NRA Accounts). Investor funds are managed through individual accounts established at Charles Schwab & Company, Inc., the largest U.S. discount broker, and specialty mutual fund companies. KCA has also negotiated to obtain specialty funds on no-load basis for it's NRA Accounts from a variety of sources. Portfolio management strategy is based on the pioneering, Nobel prize winning work of Harry Markowitz and William Sharpe. Their work emphasized risk control through diversification, and through an understanding of the relationship between risk and return. For more information on specialty portfolio managers call 1-800-678-5007.

CHAPTER SEVEN

COMING TO
AMERICA

MOVING TO
THE UNITED STATES

Many Canadians would never consider moving to the United States, while others spend thousands of dollars in their attempts to obtain legal status as U.S. residents. There are still other Canadians who live in the U.S. illegally year-round, or who stay longer than Immigration and Naturalization Service (INS) rules allow for a winter visitor. With the relative ease of crossing the border, and the ability to remain in the U.S. for extended periods of time, why should anyone consider becoming a legal resident of the United States?

For some people, United States residency means a new business opportunity. Others have had enough of giving up more than half of their earnings to high Canadian taxes; while others just prefer to live in a warmer climate. This chapter is designed to assist those people who have come to the conclusion that at some stage in their life, they might like to emigrate from Canada to the United States. Chapters 8 and 9 will help you to determine whether United States residency would be a good move financially, after taking into consideration the key cross-border issues of income tax, estate tax and medicare. For those who are seriously contemplating a move, all of the issues in this and the next two chapters need to be addressed simultaneously, for maximum benefit.

This chapter offers only a general discussion of American immigration rules and policies. Individual factors can greatly influence the course of any immigration undertaking. *Immigration can be a complex and lengthy procedure under current law, and should not be attempted without the services of a good United States immigration attorney.*

HOW TO BECOME A LEGAL RESIDENT OF THE U.S.

There are basically two normal ways to immigrate to the United States. The first is through a business or a professional relationship and the second through the sponsorship of a close family member. This is about as simple an explanation as it gets, about who is

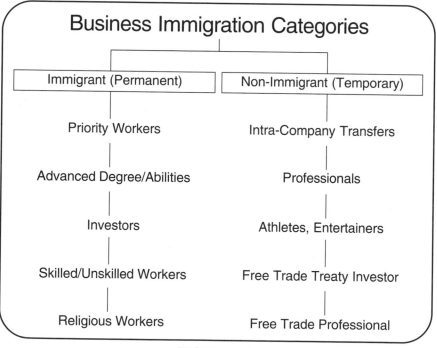

FIGURE 7.1

entitled to immigrate to the United States. After that, the whole process starts getting fairly complex and even contradictory. Figure 7.1 provides a chart of the basic business categories, under which you may acquire either a permanent or something less than permanent resident status.

As you can see from Figure 7.1, there are numerous opportunities for immigration to the United States for persons with business contacts. The business and professional immigration categories will be explained in greater detail in the next section. Where does this leave the retired person who wants to immigrate and retire in the United States Sunbelt? That's where some advance planning can pay big dividends. For those who have recently retired, or are about to retire, you should consider keeping open any business or professional relationships long enough to assist you in getting permanent immigration status. Also, those who are retired but think they wouldn't mind keeping their fingers in the business pie, investing in

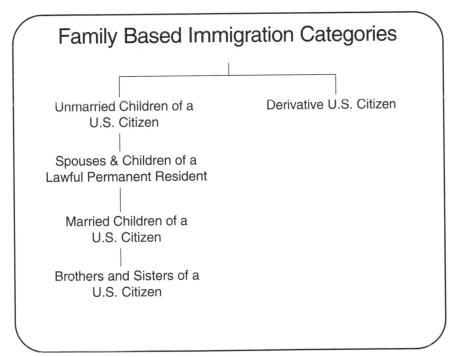

FIGURE 7.2

a small U.S. business and hiring a full time manager, can sometimes be a very suitable means to obtain a visa that allows them to legally live in the United States, year round.

For those who have no applicable business or professional means, you may wish to look for any possible family connections that may provide legal status in the United States. Figure 7.2 addresses the key family relationships that can prove useful for immigration purposes.

IMMIGRATION CATEGORIES

This section lists some of the basic qualifications for each of the business and family immigration categories that are outlined in Figures 7.1 and 7.2.

Immigrant or Lawful Permanent Resident (LPR) status is also known as a "Green Card." This status is similar to the Landed Immigrant in Canada. The Green Card is no longer even green, this year's model is really pink, or more accurately, deep salmon. Every so often, the Green Card is given a new look to impede fraudulent reproduction. Current versions of the Green Card now include an expiration date, which has not previously, ever appeared on the card. This means the card is now like a drivers license, and must be up-dated on the expiration date.

The United States Congress under President Bush, passed a major new immigration law package, which became effective in October, 1991. This new law greatly expanded the number of categories, and eligibility requirements for obtaining a Green Card. In fact, so many new Green Card categories were introduced, that the INS has had some difficulties providing proper regulations under which people can file for Green Card status. Consequently, some of the categories which are listed below, are still very much in their infancy, as far as determining how useful they may be in obtaining a Green Card.

GREEN CARD - EMPLOYMENT BASED IMMIGRANT CATEGORIES

1. **Priority Workers.** There are three priority worker classes known to the INS as EB - 1-A, 1-B, and 1-C categories:

A. Extraordinary ability immigrants in the sciences, arts, education, business and athletics. There have been no clear guidelines to date, as to what constitutes an "extraordinary" person, but someone with an advanced degree but with no special achievements in their field would likely not qualify.

B. Outstanding professors and researchers. The difference between "outstanding" and "extraordinary" is again unclear and it will be some time before this issue has been addressed, and more explicit guidelines issued by the INS.

C. Executives and managers. An executive or manager employed at least one of the three years preceding the application by the U.S. employer's Canadian affiliate, parent, subsidiary or branch office qualifies for this category. This is a very good opportunity for those business people who have a business in both Canada and the United States.

2. **Advanced Degree or Exceptional Ability Immigrants.** This category includes people with Ph.D.'s and Masters degrees. It also provides for admission of a person with exceptional ability in the arts, sciences or business. Exceptional ability like extraordinary and outstanding abilities have not been clearly defined. *This category and some other employment-based immigrant categories require labor certification.* Labor certification means before an immigrant visa can be approved, the U.S. Department of Labor must certify the offered employment position. The certification indicates there is a shortage of U.S. workers for the position offered, and there will be no adverse effect on the U.S. labor market.

Labor certification involves filing a separate application, advertising the position, recruiting prospective U.S. workers, documenting recruitment efforts and establishing final eligibility for certification.

3. **Skilled and Unskilled Workers.** This catch-all category is for immigrants with offers of employment who have been approved through Labor Certification. This category is further subdivided into:

A. Skilled workers performing a job requiring at least two years training or experience.

B. Bachelor's degreed professionals.

C. "Other workers." This sub-category is for unskilled employees.

4. **Religious Workers.** Must have been a member of and worked for a denomination for at least two years and seek entry as (a) minister (needs a baccalaureate degree); (b) religious capacity worker, or (c) other religious organization worker.

5. **Immigrant Investors.** This is sometimes referred to as the "Gold Card." It is similar to the program Canada has used for years for attracting foreign business entrepreneurs. This category is a Conditional Lawful Permanent Residence for two years until all the requirements listed below are met, then full Green Card LPR status is granted:

- Establish a new or expand an existing commercial enterprise; with an

- Investment of $500,000 (in rural or special high unemployment areas) or one million dollars in other areas that will;

- Benefit the U.S. economy; and

- Create at least 10 full time jobs for U.S. authorized workers.

EMPLOYMENT BASED NON-IMMIGRANT CATEGORIES

1. **Intra-Company Transfers.** This category is classified as the L-1 Non-immigrant Status and is good for up to seven years. This visa requires an ongoing relationship between a Canadian company and a United States parent subsidiary, branch office or affiliate. The visa applicant must be an executive or management person with specialized knowledge or training needed for the U.S. company, and the applicant must have worked for the Canadian affiliate for at least one year out of the three years prior to the transfer to the United States.

2. **Professionals and Other Temporary Workers.** This category is subdivided as the H-1 or H-1B Status and is good for up to six years. The INS publishes a list of professional occupations and other temporary workers that are in short supply and any eligible professional that has a U.S. job offer may apply for the H-1. Current occupations determined in short supply by INS are doctors, nurses and certain teachers, among others. There is no short supply list for the H1-B.

3. **Artists, Entertainers and Athletes.** There are two non-immigrant statuses available for these emigrants from Canada. These are known as the P and O Status and both are limited to the time period of a particular event(s). The O Visa is for the extraordinary artists, entertainers and athletes and is good for up to ten years (three years initially then yearly renewable thereafter) or the time period of the event(s) whichever is less. The P non-immigrant status is good for only three years extendible to five years maximum. There is a numerical cap on these visas.

4. **Canada - U.S. Free Trade Agreement Treaty Traders and Investors.** The Canadian Free Trade Agreement with the United States is the most comprehensive trade agreement between any two countries in the world. It covers the trade of goods, services, business travel, as well as investment. It was signed on January 2, 1988 and became effective

117

January 1, 1989. The Immigration Section provides for the temporary entry of business visitors, eliminates barriers to trade, facilitates across-the-border investment, provides for joint administration and dispute resolution, and emphasizes trade and the movement of people.

This means that Canadian citizens can now obtain the equivalent of E-2 visas, which are usually indefinitely renewable as long as the qualifying investment remains ongoing, and is considered the next best thing to permanent residency. Requirements for an E-2 Visa are:

• Canadian citizen.

• A substantial investment in a bona fide U.S. enterprise must be made. A substantial investment is not clearly defined but has been generally accepted as a majority ownership or investment in a business of any size, in which the investor actively participates. The amount of the investment must be an amount normally considered appropriate to establish a viable enterprise of the nature contemplated.

• The person to whom the E-2 visa will be issued must be employed in a supervisory or executive capacity or have special skills needed by the employer.

• There is no requirement for a minimum number of employees to be hired, but the number of employees required to operate the business in addition to the E-2 investor must be sufficient to make the enterprise at least marginally successful.

• The company or employer of the visa applicant must be at least 51% Canadian owned and controlled.

5. **Canada - U.S. Free Trade Agreement Professionals.** This category is a unique one and is called the TC status. It permits people to come in as non-immigrants merely on the basis of their being considered professional. No actual job offer is initially required but this TC visa must be renewed annually and will not likely be renewed if no employment is found. The list of professionals includes accountants, engineers, scientists, research assistants, medical/allied professionals, psychologists, scientific technicians, disaster

relief insurance claims adjusters, as well as other professionals such as architects, lawyers, teachers, economists, computer systems analysts, management consultants and others. Note that it omits teachers of lower grades and high school level teachers. In order to be considered a "professional" one's profession must be on the list in Schedule B of the Canada — U.S. Free Trade Agreement. Equivalence of experience will be allowed to replace educational requirements in the management consultant category only.

FAMILY BASED IMMIGRANT CATEGORIES

Family based immigration is predicated on the fact that a family member who is already a U.S. citizen or Green Card holder can sponsor other family members for permanent residence in the United States. There is also the possibility that a person looking to immigrate to the United States may already be a Derivative Citizen due to their family history. Derivative Citizenship will be covered in detail in the next section of this chapter. There are five main categories for family sponsored immigration.

The immediate relative category is separate from other family-based immigration because it is not numerically restricted. This category belongs to spouses, unmarried minor children and parents of U.S. citizens. New spouses obtaining a Green Card by marrying a U.S. citizen will receive a two year temporary Green Card and must go through an interview process after the two years before a permanent card is issued. The purpose of this process is to thwart marriages of convenience whose sole purpose is to fraudulently obtain legal immigration status. Those who saw the movie *Green Card* will have a better understanding of what this process entails with its detailed questioning of the spouses to ensure they are truly married.

In all but one of the other four categories, the family member sponsoring the Green Card LPR of another family member must be a U.S. citizen (see the section *Becoming a U.S. Citizen* later in this chapter). These categories are subject to quotas and waiting lists of a few months to several years. They work on a priority or preference system and are in order of preference:

- **1st Preference.** Unmarried sons and daughters of U.S. citizens. At the present time there is no waiting list in this category.

- **2nd Preference.** This category is broken down into two sub-categories.

A.   Spouses and minor children of Lawful Permanent Residents or Green Card holders. There is currently a wait of about 18 months in this category.

B.   Adult unmarried sons and daughters of Lawful Permanent Residents or Green Card holders. There is a waiting period of 18 months in this category.

- **3rd Preference.** Married children of U.S. citizens. There a waiting period in this category of about eight months.

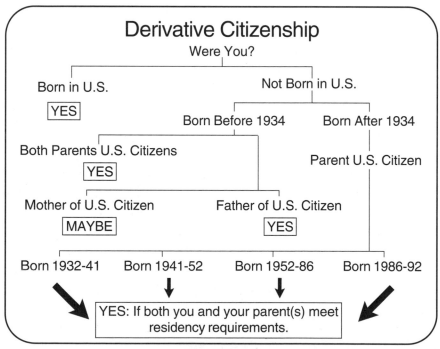

FIGURE 7.3

- **4th Preference.** Siblings of U.S. citizens. There is a waiting period in this category of about ten years. Even though the waiting list may be quite long it is worthwhile getting on this list as a change in legislation could either reduce the waiting period, and/ or increase quotas, and people already on the list could move much more quickly.

DERIVATIVE CITIZENSHIP - ARE YOU A U.S. CITIZEN?

With Canada and the United States being so closely related in geography and past history, there has been a substantial migration of residents back and forth across the 49th parallel. As a result, many Canadians, although they may never have lived in the United States, may actually be a U.S. citizen solely because of their ancestry. *This is what is known as Derivative Citizenship, obtaining U.S. citizenship by a form of inheritance or derivation.*

Derivative citizenship was first established into law by the United States Congress in the late seventeen hundreds. Since then, Congress has amended the rules as to who is eligible for derivative citizenship status, at least a dozen times. Consequently, the rules to determine derivative citizenship can be quite complex.

Figure 7.3 illustrates a possible flow chart about how one can determine whether they are a U.S. citizen. The YES or MAYBE notations indicate possible derivative citizenship, if all other qualifications are met as outlined in Figure 7.3.

The flow chart on Figure 7.3 gives you some indication about who may qualify as a derivative citizen, but with the twelve or more Congressional amendments to the citizenship rules, it becomes a very complex issue. For example, it is conceivable one member of a family acquired U.S. citizenship on their day of birth, while a later born sibling is out of luck. After May 24, 1934, U.S. residency of the U.S. citizen ancestor becomes a vital ingredient in establishing American citizenship entitlement. In addition, during certain periods of time, Congress required the potential derivative citizen to have some residency requirements. Figure 7.3 is further explained in the following summary:

Born In The U.S. If you were born in the United States you have likely retained your U.S. citizenship, unless you have actively done something to renounce it. Prior to 1990, a United States born person taking up citizenship, or even just voting in another country, was considered to have renounced their U.S. citizenship. Since then, the State Department has published new guidelines to determine retention of U.S. citizenship: they now presume a person intends to retain U.S. citizenship, even though that person obtains naturalization in, or declares allegiance to another country. This new policy is retroactive. *This means that it applies to people who think they may have lost their U.S. citizenship; even if the U.S. Consulate has already made a negative finding.*

Both Parents are U.S. Citizens. If both your parents are U.S. citizens, you will generally have a claim to U.S. citizenship, particularly if one or both of your parents ever resided in the United States. This applies even if you have never lived in the U.S.

Born before May 24, 1934. If you were born before this date and your father was a U.S. citizen, you are eligible for U.S. citizenship. Under current law, citizenship cannot be transferred from a U.S. citizen mother. This has recently been found inequitable by the United States courts and there is proposed legislation before Congress to rectify the situation. A change in legislation is expected soon.

Born May 15, 1932 to November 13, 1941. Canadians born in this time frame are subject to two conditions. First, the U.S. citizen parent must have had a prior U.S. residency. Second, the would-be derivative citizen must retain his citizenship through a two-year continuous presence (although not necessarily an uninterrupted stay) in the United States. The terms residency and presence have no clear definition, but are interpreted through facts and circumstances and prior case law.

Born November 13, 1941 to December 24, 1952. Similar to those Canadians in the prior category, the prospective derivative citizen and his U.S. parent are subject to residency requirements. Here, the U.S. parent must have ten years U.S. residency, at least five of which were after age 16. The two year continuous presence requirement for the potential derivative citizen is also in force.

Born December 24, 1952 to November 13, 1986. If you were born in this time period, your U.S. parent must have been physically present in the U.S. ten years, at least five of which were after age 14. After October 10, 1978, the retention through residency requirement for the potential derivative citizen was abolished.

Born Since November 13, 1986. The U.S. parent must have five years of prior physical presence in the United States, at least two of which were after age fourteen in order to transmit citizenship. No residency is required of the prospective derivative citizen.

After establishing that you are eligible for derivative citizenship, the biggest and most rewarding challenge comes from documenting the facts of the U.S. parent's relationship and residency. Prospective derivative citizens sometimes need to become ancestral detectives; searching through old family and government records to shed new light on their past. Family bibles, voter registrations, census records, sworn statements of family members, all have been used successfully to establish entitlement for U.S. citizenship status.

APPLYING FOR U.S. CITIZENSHIP

United States Citizenship is acquired through three methods:

- Birth.
- Derivation.
- Naturalization.

Obtaining citizenship by birth and derivation were explained in the previous section on *Derivative Citizenship*. You may apply for, or confirm your citizenship status by either completing a Form N-600 with the INS or simply submitting an application for a passport to the United States State Department. Most people will find the passport route the quickest and most hassle-free method of confirming your United States citizenship status. The State Department is not nearly as bogged down as the INS in other immigration issues, and if you are turned down you will know about it much earlier, and you can begin the appeals process that much sooner, if you feel you have a legitimate claim.

Acquiring U.S. citizenship by naturalization is available to those who have a five-year continuous legal permanent residence in the United States. In other words, you must have had a Green Card and been physically present in the United States without any interruptions over six months for five years. Those who are married to a U.S. citizen have only a three year continuous residency requirement. For naturalization, one needs to demonstrate physical presence for the required amount of time; good moral character; minimum knowledge of English, U.S. history and government.

Naturalization is a relatively simple process which begins with submitting application Form N-400 to the INS, along with a $90.00 fee, two color photographs and a set of fingerprints. The most difficult question on Form N-400 is providing the details of every trip you took outside of the United States since you received your Green Card. There is an oral examination scheduled within four months after filing the N-400 to prove U.S. and English knowledge and verify eligibility for U.S. citizenship. Shortly after a successful examination, a U.S. District Court Judge will confer citizenship at a swearing-in ceremony.

Whether American citizenship is acquired through birth, naturalization or derivation, it can provide the ease of U.S. access many Canadians seek. We remind those who are considering United States immigration or citizenship to use the services of a competent cross-border financial planner to address the tax consequences of such a move *before* they occur.

DUAL CITIZENSHIP - IS IT POSSIBLE?

There are few issues -- outside of which way the Canadian dollar is going, that are more hotly debated by Canadians in the United States, than whether one is, or can become, a dual citizen of Canada and the United States.

To begin with, there *is* such a thing as dual citizenship, even though you will have a difficult time finding an immigration official in either Canada or the United States who can tell you anything about it, let alone admit that it exists. There is no formal procedure to apply for dual citizenship. You basically acquire it by applying for U.S. Citizenship, and not relinquishing your Canadian Citizenship.

Dual citizenship exists for Canadian citizens under two basic fact patterns. First, there is the case where a Canadian Green Card holder -- Lawful Permanent Resident of the U.S. becomes a naturalized U.S. citizen. Since 1977, Canada has not revoked its citizenship upon the U.S. naturalization of its citizens. Consequently, the Canadian holds citizenship status in both countries. Secondly, a Canadian born person who meets the criteria for a United States derivative citizenship status as outlined earlier in this Chapter can have, and hold both a Canadian and United States passport at the same time. As a result, they are a dual citizen as well.

Dual citizenship does not come from any formal application for "dual citizenship" but by default. Consequently, individuals calling the United States Immigration and Naturalization Service Offices, or even Canadian Consulates in the United States inquiring about how they can apply for dual citizenship, get a series of blank stares and/or negative responses.

So, you can currently achieve dual citizenship if you are a Canadian citizen who qualifies for U.S. citizenship, by simply applying for the United States citizenship and not formally renouncing your Canadian citizenship. Your new Canadian passport will indicate your dual status inside the passport. The United States basically ignores the fact that someone applying for American citizenship would want to keep the citizenship of another country at the same time, and does nothing to formally recognize or deny this dual status situation. The reluctance of the INS to accept dual citizenship may stem from fear of divided loyalties and citizenship by convenience.

The Canadian/U.S. dual citizen is envied for having the best of both worlds, and is in no way restricted from living, working or vacationing in either country for any reason for their entire lives. In addition these dual citizens can pass this on to their children.

THE GREEN CARD LOTTERY

From time to time, the United States Congress allows for an Immigrant Visa Lottery. This is a free lottery, which offers a large number of visas on a random determinant with no employment or family based qualifications required. Congress decides from which countries it will take entries based on which countries they feel have not gotten a fair stake in the immigrant categories through the normal visa process and other political reasons.

In 1992 and 1993 Congress held two separate lotteries of 50,000 applicants each. Canadians were included as eligible for bulk lotteries. There are no future lotteries scheduled for 1994 or future years to date. Typically, the entry process is made public several months before the drawings are made and each person is allowed only one application. Spouses however, may each file separate entries.

The entries are very simple to complete, and contrary to advertisements from immigration services, you do not need to pay, nor do you gain advantage, from having someone prepare and submit your application.

Your entry must be typed and will require only the following information:

- Name of applicant
- Date of birth.
- Place of birth. (City, Province and Country)
- Names, dates and places of birth of the applicant's spouse and minor children.
- Current mailing address and location of the nearest U.S. Consular's office or, if you are already in the United States, your most recent foreign address before entry. (The United States Consulates in Canada are listed in Appendix D)

Once your entry has been typed with the information required, it should be placed in an envelope no larger than 9 1/2 by 4 1/2 inches (24 cm by 11 cm) and no smaller than 6 by 3 1/2 inches (15 cm by 9 cm). Canada must be typed on the front upper left hand corner of the envelope. The completed application is to be mailed to the United States State Department. The exact mailing address will be announced well before the lottery drawing, along with dates before and after which no entries will be accepted. Call your nearest U.S. Consulate for the dates of the lottery. Also, any good immigration attorney's office will probably supply you with this information in the hopes that you will refer them future immigration work.

LEGAL RETIREMENT IN THE UNITED STATES

Even though statistics show large numbers of Canadians spending much of their retirement in the Sunbelt, there is no such thing as a retiree's visa. A separate visa category for retirees did exist, but it was closed down in the mid 1970's, due to some changes in U.S. immigration rules. There is a move a foot by at least one key U.S. Senator to bring back this retirement visa, because of the obvious economic benefits to the Sunbelt States. However, all immigration policy is a political football and it is difficult to predict how soon, if at all, any form of retirement visa will again be available This surprises many Canadians who do not intend to create any burden whatsoever, upon the U.S. economy.

How then, can you legally retire in the U.S.? In this chapter we have covered many immigration options, all of which apply to anyone regardless of whether they are officially retired or not. In spite of this, most Canadian retirees or business persons probably travel to the U.S. as temporary visitors. Because of the relationship between Canada and the United States, entering each others country as a visitor is free from any formalities, even though there are certain requirements which must be followed.

There are really two types of non-immigrant status for these people: visitors for business, and visitors for pleasure. Visitors for business are B-1 visitors. Visitors for pleasure are B-2 visitors. The INS normally allows Canadians six months when they enter on this temporary visitor status. The B-1 and B-2 visas for Canadians require no formal application or documentation. All that's required to be allowed into the United States on this status is a simple statement with respect to the time and purpose of your visit. Under the Free Trade Agreement, Canadians can get a document showing temporary visitor for business status for a period of one year.

Although B-1 and B-2 Visas only allow you to remain in the United States for six months, there is no prohibition against leaving the country and re-entering, even if it's only a day trip to Mexico. In Chapter 1, we discussed the differences between being a legal resident of the United States for tax purposes and immigration purposes. Consequently, leaving the United States after six months as a visitor, and then re-entering may work fine for immigration purposes, but subject you to a whole new set of tax rules as the protection from taxation under the Canada — U.S. Tax Treaty no longer applies. Refer back to Chapter 3, for more on the tax implications of remaining in the U.S. for more than six months a year.

As a temporary visitor, the retiree or business visitor must maintain a residence in Canada, because he or she cannot intend to reside permanently in the United States.

CANADIAN RESIDENTS HOLDING GREEN CARDS

It is estimated that thousands of Canadians, who currently reside in Canada, also hold Green Card LPR status in the United States, because of previous employment, more open immigration policies or the immigrant lottery. Often, these persons are not sure what they should do with their Green Cards -- whether they should leave them in the drawer, move to the United States, throw it away, or get in touch with the INS for direction.

The bottom line is that anyone holding a Green Card under these circumstances, needs to carefully consider their options before deciding whether to use it or lose it.

In strict technical terms, when a Green Card holder takes up permanent residency outside the United States, they have abandoned their LPR Green Card status. In actuality, they still are in possession of the Green Card, and could use it to take up full-time residency in the United States, as long as they appeared in all respects to be a United States resident. Some Canadians, have had their cards seized when entering the United States, because they gave immigration officials reason to believe that they were no longer a permanent resident of the United States.

Keeping your Green Card active entitles you to all its privileges such as being able to live and work year round in the United States. On the other hand, a Green Card comes with corresponding responsibilities like filing tax returns and maintaining a presence in the United States. The tax consequences of holding a Green Card are discussed in Chapter 3 and the tax advantages given in Chapter 8. Since it is very difficult for most people to obtain a Green Card, Canadian residents who have one should carefully consider all their options before making any decision. There is no real middle ground here, as the INS allows no lengthy stays outside the United States without having to meet admission criteria for re-entry. *The only real way to keep your Green Card is to use it.* The following guidelines should help guide those who wish to maintain their Green Card LPR:

- Use your Green Card every time you enter the U.S.

- Maintain clear evidence of residence. For example, file U.S. Income Tax Returns, use a U.S. drivers license and vehicle registration, keep U.S. bank and investment accounts --- all with a United States address.

- Keep Alien Resident Card information current. You can update by filing Form I-90 if name changes or Form AR-11 for change of address.

- Ensure trips to Canada or abroad don't exceed one year from your last U.S. entry date. (If you anticipate an absence from the U.S. in excess of one year, obtain a Re-entry Permit (INS Form I-131) before leaving. Re-entry Permits are valid for a maximum of two years and cannot be renewed).

If, after weighing all the factors you are certain there will be no advantages to your keeping your Green Card, you should mail it to any United States Consulate office, or surrender it next time you cross the border.

MARRIAGE TO A U.S. CITIZEN

We were cautious about calling them mixed marriages, but there are probably thousands of Canadians who marry American citizens every year. Many of these are second marriages, because respective spouses have been widowed by their previous partners.

These marriages will trigger several important decisions that cannot be ignored without some major tax problems or missed opportunities. Some of the issues facing these cross-border couples are:

- Where do they, as a couple actually reside?

- Where and how do they file tax returns for their maximum advantage?

- How do they revise their estate plan to fit a cross-border situation that avoids double estate taxation, and takes advantage of all available deductions?

- How do they maximize government benefits like CPP, OAS, Social Security and U.S. or Canadian medicare?

- How do they merge the two separate families in the two countries into their own personal goals, financial or otherwise?

All of the these issues are covered indirectly through discussions in other chapters. This section will attempt to put them all into focus. Cross-border marriages may be a common occurrence, but there is little assistance available, and a great need for cross-border financial planning.

The first area of concern is which country to call home. As a married couple, it becomes largely a matter of choice. The Canadian citizen spouse can sponsor the U.S. citizen spouse for Landed Immigrant status in Canada, or the U.S. citizen spouse can sponsor the Canadian citizen spouse for a Green Card into the United States. The third option is for each spouse to remain a resident of their original country, and a non-resident of their spouse's country. This option presents some unique difficulties, and is recommended only in unusual circumstances, and only then, on a short term basis.

Many couples in similar situations make their decisions based on the economic realities of where they can get the best bottom line results from their combined financial resources. The major issues to consider here, are income and estate taxes, medical coverage, and the cost of living.

The cost of living is generally accepted to be lower, to substantially lower in the United States. Depending on life-style, some large savings can be achieved by a couple spending the majority of their time in the United States.

Income taxes are covered in great detail in both Chapters 3 and 8. Estate tax issues are discussed in Chapters 4 and 8. Chapters 5 and 9 cover medicare, medical insurance, and the entitlements to government sponsored programs such as U.S. Social Security, Canada Pension Plan and Old Age Security.

Even after reviewing all the issues in the previous chapters, and making the appropriate calculations, it should be abundantly clear that there is no good answer as to where a Canadian - American couple should reside. It really depends on personal preference, along with a combination of all the other factors, as applied to your own personal situation. A complete cross-border financial planning analysis can help you determine the financial implications of either move. *The assistance of a cross-border financial planner is recommended for couples in this situation and his guidance should result in a good return on the investment of time and money.*

WHAT TO DO IF YOU ARE REFUSED ENTRY TO THE U.S.

A traveller's greatest fear crossing an international border, is being hassled by some overly officious immigration officer. Many of you have heard stories about friends or relatives being detained, or turned away for no apparent reason. Perhaps their vacation plans were ruined because an immigration officer misinterpreted an innocent remark. Some of you, may have even had this happen to you. Are you really defenseless against the onslaught of a border guard who is just having a bad day? Absolutely not! Here are some things you can do, to ease your exits and entries to and from the

United States, and eliminate some the stresses involved with dealing with immigration. When entering the United States:

- Have proper personal identification, we recommend Canadians have at least one of the following: A valid provincial drivers license, birth certificate and a passport.

- If you have a Green Card or other United States visa, produce them to the immigration official.

- If you are a visitor to the United States, be prepared to provide proof that you intend to return to Canada, for example return tickets and proof of a Canadian residence, bank accounts etc.

- If you are refused entry to the United States, and can't see any quick resolution ask for a deferred ruling to the nearest INS office in the United States where you will be staying. You will likely be allowed to enter the United States until a hearing is set up, and you will get to present your case in a more favorable environment. You will also have the time to engage an immigration attorney.

CROSS-BORDER Q&A

Many of the issues covered in the preceding chapter of this book have already been touched upon in the *Cross Border Q & A* column which appears in *The Sun Times of Canada,* and the author's own newsletter *The Sunbelt Canadian.* A majority of these questions have been posed by readers, looking for advice relating to their own specific problems or situations. At the end of each chapter, we have included some typical reader questions, along with our response, to better illustrate and flesh out the concepts presented in the chapter.

Obtaining a Green Card

We are retired and financially independent Canadians and we want to retire in Arizona. What are our chances of immigrating to the U.S.? What is a "Green Card" and how do we get one? Does it help that I have a brother who is a Green Card holder and living in Florida?

— Jacques S., Phoenix, AZ

There are two basic ways of immigrating to the United States. One is to achieve permanent resident status through a job, and the other, is through a relative. There are other ways as well, but these can involve lengthy court proceedings. In your case, since your brother already has a Green Card, immigration through a relative seems like the better possibility. However, a lawful permanent resident (or Green Card holder), cannot petition for his siblings. He must become a United States citizen to do so. Citizenship normally requires five years of permanent residence, unless the permanent residence was acquired through a United States citizen spouse, in which case the permanent resident need only wait three years before filing his application for U.S. citizenship.

Once sworn in as a United States citizen, your brother may immediately file a visa petition for you in the category of "forth preference." The date of filing becomes your "priority date" as far as the wait associated with most preference visa categories. At the current time, the "quota wait" for forth preference for Canada is April 1, 1982. This means that those beneficiaries of visa petitions which were filed on April 1, 1982 are eligible for admission to the U.S.

Derivative Citizenship

My parents were U.S. citizens, but I was born in Canada and have lived there all my life. I am 65. Could I obtain U.S. citizenship easily if I want to? Similarly, my wife, who is 59, also had U.S. citizens as parents. Would it be any easier for her to get U.S. citizenship?

— *Duane E., Scottsdale, AZ*

One or both of you may already be United States citizens. You must prove your derivative citizenship by filing Form N-600, "Application for Certificate of Citizenship," along with supporting documentation with the Immigration and Naturalization Service (INS).

Since you both were born before 1934, citizenship could only have been transmitted by your fathers in your case (unless Congress passes pending legislation allowing citizenship prior to this date to be passed through the mother also).

This means that you must discover if your fathers ever knowingly abandoned their United States citizenships prior to your birth, by taking an oath of allegiance to the government of Canada, and forswearing allegiances to all other nations.

In the event documentary evidence is lacking for one of your derivative citizenship claims, all is not lost. It would only be necessary for one of you to prove U.S. citizenship. Then the other could immigrate as the immediate relative of the United States citizen, a category for which there is no quota wait.

Overstaying Your Welcome

How many days can I stay in the U.S. each year without applying to the INS for an extension? What are the legal consequences if I stay for a few days longer than I am supposed to?

— Chuck F., Palm Springs, CA

This is a rather broad question. The broad answer is, that it depends upon the circumstances under which you entered the United States. For example, if you entered for a temporary period on a wave and a smile at the border (which is allowed for Canadian visitors), you can stay six months. Since you have no I-94 (temporary Visa document) to extend, the honor system is used for your departure. There is no formal extension procedure. Of course, you may stay only as a business visitor or as a tourist. You must not be employed, or establish permanent residence in the U.S.

Hiring an Immigration Attorney

When should I use an attorney to help me immigrate to the U.S.? What would it cost relative to my status? How long does it take?

— Ward C., Tucson, AZ

There is no law that says immigration documents may not be filed by an individual. However, there may be alternatives available to you that you may only find out about through a consultation with an attorney. Certainly, if you become involved in a problem with the Immigration Service, you would be well advised to get professional assistance immediately. Most immigration attorneys work on an hourly basis.

Immigration Strategies and the Need for Financial Planning

I read your articles in the Sun Times of Canada, and have the following questions regarding cross-border financial planning and immigration. My husband and I wish to immigrate to the U.S. My husband is a civil technologist currently employed by a road construction firm. I run my own advertising/promotions firm, registered as an Ontario Corporation.

1. How can we immigrate with a minimum of fuss and expense? (I have heard rumors about bringing in $100,000 and hiring one employee.) What are the costs involved? Also, my husband's sister has lived and worked in Michigan for the last 15 years. If she becomes an American citizen, could she sponsor us, and could we both get jobs and work? How long would it take for her to get U.S. citizenship and sponsor us?

2. Would it be to our greater advantage to procure jobs in order to immigrate? Or, is it a disadvantage to me, especially since I have an existing corporation?

3. If we are no longer Canadian residents, I assume there are tax advantages, (no dual tax) but does this lack of residency affect our current investments i.e. our family home (must we sell), our RRSP's held in a Canadian brokerage house, our life insurance held by Canadian firms, etc.

— *Lita P., Toronto, ON*

1. From what you have told us, the best alternative for you to immigrate to the U.S., would likely be through your business of advertising/promotion. By forming a similar business in the U.S., this business would then be the means for you to qualify for a Visa under Treaty Investor Route (E-2) or a regular inter-company transfer (L-1), or even the new Green Card category (EIC) for established businesses similar to the L-1.

The E-2 is likely the quickest and easiest to achieve. Many good immigration attorneys recommend you invest $100,000 or more in the U.S. business to qualify for this type of visa. However, Arizona immigration attorneys working for our clients in non-capital intensive service industries similar to your business, have gotten E-2 visas for investments of less than $10,000. Even though there is no requirement to hire U.S. workers, the more employment you can create, and the more capital you have to back up your business, the better off you are.

The best long term route if you can swing it, is the Green Card route through a transfer from your established Canadian Company to your U.S. affiliated company which you would set up. The Green Card is a permanent residency status, whereas all the other visas may be subject to continuing requirements and/or have expiration dates. In addition, the Green Card is the only route that will give your husband the ability to work in the U.S., without separately qualifying for a visa under the same rules as yourself.

Your husband's sister can become a naturalized U.S. citizen if she has had her green card for 5 years or more. It is currently taking 3-8 months, from date of application, to complete this process. Once she is a citizen she can sponsor your husband for permanent resident status (or Green Card). However, there is a waiting list in this category of nearly ten years. It wouldn't hurt to get on this waiting list as sometimes quotas are changed, and the waiting list can disappear, or at least be shortened.

As you can see, the maze of rules and regulations can be overwhelming and I recommend you use a good immigration attorney located in the area which you are likely to relocate in the U.S. Be prepared to spend $2,000 - $4,000 on legal fees to get the job done for you and your husband. If you are well organized and can do a lot of the necessary work yourself, the legal fees could be lower, but they will increase if you do not have a concrete plan of action, that you can outline to the attorney.

2. You will not legally be able to procure employment in the U.S. unless you have a visa or have some special skills/education that allows you a work visa, based on these exceptional qualifications. If you have a Ph.D. or other post secondary degree(s) or equivalent experience, your immigration attorney will direct you to these special categories.

3. As far as your taxes and other financial matters are concerned, there are some good planning opportunities and there are some pitfalls. These are difficult to condense into this type of response and require a great deal of factual analysis. To assure you maximize the opportunities and avoid the pitfalls, I recommend you complete a comprehensive financial plan, with the assistance of a professional planner that is knowledgeable in both Canadian and U.S. tax, investment, estate and insurance requirements.

Hiring a Lawyer for Green Card Lottery

My wife and I are very interested in moving to the USA as permanent residents. We are in our late fifties, retired, British and Canadian citizens, own property in Florida and Ontario, and are financially secure. At present, we split our time between Canada and the United States, but we both feel that we would prefer to settle permanently in Florida, if at all possible. Last fall, we entered into the "Green Card" lottery that was held in America, guided by a lawyer in Toronto who charged us $400.00, but of course we have not been successful. He has not even had the courtesy to let us know any results. We would appreciate any advice that you can give us in our quest to live in America. I might also point out that I do not intend to seek work here, and we will want to get the best medical insurance coverage. Thank you in anticipation.

— Paul C., Sarasota, FL

We get a large number of inquiries similar to your dilemma. Unfortunately, there are currently only two major ways to get a U.S. immigration status and that is through Family Sponsorship or a Business/Employment Sponsorship.

It sounds like you have no family situations that may help, but it is worth checking on the birth places of your parents, grandparents or even great grandparents, to see if there is any derivative citizenship in your family history.

If you had some outstanding achievements, awards and/or attained higher levels of education, you may be able to pursue a Green Card without having any employment requirements, under the new extraordinary or outstanding alien applicant categories.

Other than those suggestions, the annual lottery, which Canada will be included in the fall of 1992 and 1993, may be your only hope unless you decided to buy a small business and get a visa under the Canada/U.S. Free Trade Agreement.

I'm sorry, but you wasted your $400 on the attorney. The State Department only requires that you provide a typed list of your name, address, date of birth, place of birth and include the same information for your spouse and dependent children for the Visa Lottery. This is not something you need to pay an attorney for.

In your own best interest, I encourage you to ask your Senators and Congressmen in Florida for their support of a bill that is currently being sponsored by Senator DeConcini of Arizona. This bill would allow retired persons such as yourself, a visa to retire in the United States, providing they could prove financial self sufficiency, and that they did not intend to work in the United States.

This bill would be a win win situation for both the United States and the immigrant. The United States would get a new tax payer at no cost, who would create jobs through spending on goods and services, and the immigrant would get a permanent place in the Sun Belt.

Is U.S. Citizenship Required for Estate Tax Exemptions?

You mentioned in a previous article that dual citizenship exists, and that Canada does not revoke citizenship if one chooses to become a U.S. citizen. Does the U.S. also allow a U.S. citizen to remain a citizen of Canada?

My husband and I are both Canadian citizens by birth who became permanent U.S. residents and Green Card holders in 1977. We live permanently in Florida. Our problem is whether or not to become U.S. citizens to take advantage of the $600,000 exemption from estate tax, since you mentioned that only U.S. citizens can take full advantage of this exemption.

— *Mary S., North Miami, FL*

It is Canada's choice, whether or not you keep your Canadian citizenship. Only the country conferring citizenship on an individual can require that person to relinquish prior citizenship. For the time being Canada allows individuals to retain Canadian citizenship after becoming a U.S. citizen.

Since you are a Green Card holder domiciled in the U.S. you already qualify for the $600,000 estate tax exemption and so does your husband. You do not have to become U.S. citizens to qualify for these exemptions.

By becoming a U.S. citizen you gain the ability to defer estate tax on estates over $600,000 to the second spouse's death by using the unlimited marital deduction. You may use a Qualified Domestic Trust to take advantage of the unlimited marital deduction as an alternative to becoming a citizen.

If you or your husband's estate(s) are over $600,000 you need to seriously consider your options with the help of a professional estate planner; if you still have assets in Canada you'll need a cross-border estate planner.

The Real Deal on Dual Citizenship

I am confused about your statement regarding dual citizenship in the Sun Times. I have it on good authority that dual citizenship is possible only under very extenuating circumstances in the United States. Would you kindly tell me the real facts on this issue.

— *Richard Y., Venice, FL*

There are few issues outside of which way the Canadian dollar is going, that are more hotly debated by Canadians in the United States, than whether one is or can become a dual citizen of Canada and the United States.

To start off, there is such a thing as dual citizenship. I am a Canadian citizen myself and have become a United States citizen. Because Canada does not require me to give up my Canadian citizenship, I am a dual citizen. In my practice, I have recommended and assisted several clients to become dual citizens and know personally of many others.

139

Dual citizenship comes not from any formal application for "dual citizenship" but by default. Consequently, individuals calling the United States Immigration and Naturalization Service Offices, in particular, or even Canadian Consulates in the United States inquiring on how they can qualify for or apply for Dual Citizenship, get a series of blank stares and/or negative responses.

Since 1977, Canada has stopped demanding that Canadians who emigrate and who take up foreign citizenship, to give up their Canadian citizenship. There are only a few other countries in the world that have the same policy such as the United Kingdom and Israel. The United States does not allow its citizens to hold United States citizenship if they become citizens of another country.

So you can currently achieve dual citizenship if you are a Canadian citizen by simply applying for United States citizenship and not formally doing anything to renounce your Canadian citizenship. Your new Canadian passport will indicate your dual status. The United States does nothing to formally recognize a dual status situation, and ignores that fact that someone applying for U.S. citizenship is retaining the citizenship of the other country.

Dual Citizenship for Naturalized Canadians

I am a Canadian citizen who worked in the United States for 15 years. We eventually moved to Canada in 1967, and in 1972, my wife became a Canadian citizen. I recall you telling a lady in similar circumstances that she had dual citizenship. Would this also apply to my wife as well? I have heard so many stories on this subject, and thought that perhaps, you could set the record straight.

— *Arthur T., Clearwater, FL*

From the previous question you can see that it is more difficult for a United States citizen to become a dual citizen. Your wife gave up her United States citizenship when she became a Canadian citizen. She may get her U.S. citizenship back by convincing the INS that she did not intend to give up that citizenship when she became a Canadian. We have been able to resurrect several U.S. citizenships this way, working with good immigration attorneys. I recommend the use of a U.S. Immigration attorney, before attempting this.

CHAPTER EIGHT

THE GRASS IS
ALWAYS GREENER

CANADIAN VS. U.S.
TAXATION POLICIES

O ne of the major considerations for anyone considering a move
to the United States is how much income tax they may be
able to save. Many Canadians are frustrated by the seeming-
ly endless spiral of federal and provincial taxes, PST, GST and
property taxes. Most Canadians accept higher taxes as the price of
Canada's superior social welfare system, but recent tax increases
have come with a commensurate decrease in government services.
Have Canadians lost confidence in the politicians who have created
this monster, and who now seem incapable of doing anything about
it? *This may be why some Canadians have voted with their feet, by
moving to the United States, and voting themselves a major tax cut.*

This chapter will address those tax saving opportunities, and
will provide a good guideline for those Canadians who may be
derivative citizens of the United States, or have other immigration
possibilities. It is for those who may be looking for some financial
advantage, by becoming a resident of the United States for tax
purposes. Chapter 9 will discuss the opportunities in investments,
medical coverage, insurance and U.S. Social Security benefits.

In Chapter 3, under the heading of *Canada — United States Income Tax Comparison,* we outlined some of the basic tax rates and tax deduction comparisons between the United States and Canada. We will now incorporate these comparisons into a cross-border financial plan using the perspective of someone who is actually moving or contemplating a move to the United States. We will use real examples of how particular Canadians have effectively been able to utilize cross-border financial planning, to maximize the benefits while minimizing the pitfalls when moving south.

First, our discussion will look at a line by line analysis of each type of taxable income and deduction, and then we will tie it all together using full comprehensive case studies of Canadians who have gone through professional cross-border financial planning.

GET 50% OF YOUR CPP TAX FREE & AVOID OAS CLAWBACK

A popular misconception among Canadians, is that they lose CPP and/or OAS benefits after exiting Canada. *In fact, the opposite is true and they will actually receive more of their benefits on an after tax basis.* The Canada — United States Tax Treaty provides for some very interesting tax advantages for those Canadians who are collecting or are eligible for CPP and Old Age Security.

Because of provisions contained in the treaty, one half of both your CPP and OAS are completely free from taxation, when you file tax returns in the United States. The other half of this income is taxed at the applicable United States rates, which as you can see from Figure 3.2 are much lower to begin with.

In addition, a Canadian resident of the United States is not subject to the OAS clawback. Let's look at a real example of what this one item can mean to George, who moves from Ottawa to the United States with $6,500 of CPP and $4,500 of OAS benefits. George, and his wife Susan, are both retired in the maximum Canadian tax bracket and are subject to the OAS clawback if they remain in Canada. (All dollar amounts in Figure 8.1 through 8.8 are in Canadian funds, and we have used the tax rates from Figure 3.2)

As you can see from Figure 8.1, George would see a drop in his average tax rate from 72%, to a maximum of 16% on this combination of CPP and OAS income, by moving to the United States. The resulting tax savings of $6,240 is significant, especially when you consider George's wife is in a similar situation. Their combined savings would be doubled to $12,480. *So, before George and his wife Susan even consider any other potential tax reductions on investment and other pension income, they are set for a raise of over $1,000 per month.*

INTEREST INCOME - TAX FREE IF YOU WISH

In the United States, there is a form of local government bonds called Municipal Bonds, which pay interest free from income tax at both the federal and state levels. These are the bonds cities use to build public buildings, roads, airports and hospitals. As a result,

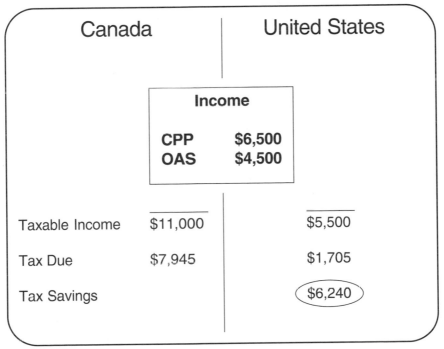

Canada	United States

Income	
CPP	$6,500
OAS	$4,500

	Canada	United States
Taxable Income	$11,000	$5,500
Tax Due	$7,945	$1,705
Tax Savings		$6,240

FIGURE 8.1

someone earning a great deal of interest income can, in effect, zero out the tax liability on any amount of interest they earn, by using these municipal bonds. Some forms of these bonds may be subject to U.S. alternative minimum tax. But, when you consider interest in Canada is taxed at full rates of up to 50% or more, in some provinces, a zero tax rate looks pretty attractive. However, from an investment planning aspect (see Chapter 9) it is not wise to throw all of your eggs into one basket, and place the majority of your investments into municipal bonds, or any other asset class for that matter. In addition, municipal bonds pay lower rates of interest, and that must also be taken into consideration. For example, these bonds are currently paying around 5% compared to about 6% on Canadian term deposits or GICs. If you are in a 50% income tax bracket, you will keep only 3% of the 6% you earned on a GIC, so a 5% rate on a tax free bond would still yield 40% more. In fact, at maximum Canadian tax rates, you would have to earn 10% or better, to net the same amount, on an after tax basis, as the 5% tax free municipal bond.

In various federal budgets over the past ten years, the Canadian Parliament has gradually eliminated the ability to defer income taxes on Canada Savings Bonds, annuities and long term GICs. This means all interest earned on any investment must be paid on a current annual basis and cannot be deferred to a later date when the interest is actually received. For anyone saving for their future retirement, the ability to defer paying income tax to some future date, particularly when they may be in a lower tax bracket, can increase their total return quite dramatically. For example, if you had $100,000, earning 10% interest over 15 years and were in a 50% tax bracket, you could net $158,682 of earnings after tax, if you could defer paying the tax until the fifteenth year. You would net only $107,893 if you had to pay the tax on a current or accrual basis under the present Canadian tax rules. *This is an over 47% increase in income from a basic investment.* It is for this reason that RRSP's work so well over the long haul, because in addition to getting a deduction for your contribution, the interest and other income accumulates tax free. *This ability to defer tax on interest in the United States is not limited to RRSP-like investments, and the taxpayer can deposit unlimited sums into investment vehicles that will allow for tax free compounding and deferment of interest, dividends and capital gains for any period of years.* We repeat however, that it would not be prudent to place all ones investments into tax free or tax deferred investments from an investment or an estate planning stand point.

Let's call on George and Susan again, to look at the interest income portion of their tax picture, and then compare their tax savings potential of moving to the United States. In the example used in Figure 8.2, we make the assumption that they have $150,000 of investments in interest bearing vehicles such as bonds and GICs, earning an average rate of interest of 9% for a total of $13,500. After moving to the United States, they decide to split their portfolio into 1/3 tax free municipal bonds earning 6% or $3,000, 1/3 tax deferred annuities earning 9% or $4,500 and leave the remaining 1/3 in investments similar to their Canadian portfolio earning 9% or $4,500. Amounts in Figure 8.2 are shown in Canadian funds.

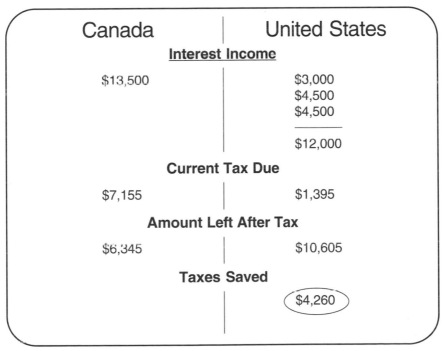

Canada	United States
Interest Income	
$13,500	$3,000
	$4,500
	$4,500
	$12,000
Current Tax Due	
$7,155	$1,395
Amount Left After Tax	
$6,345	$10,605
Taxes Saved	
	$4,260

FIGURE 8.2

In the Figure 8.2 example, George and Susan's interest income, after current taxes are paid, is over 60% larger. It should be noted that the 1/3 of the investment portfolio in the tax deferred annuity will be subject to tax when withdrawn at some future date. However, as we have previously mentioned, taxes deferred can be taxes saved. In the 31% tax bracket, they only have to defer the payment of tax for approximately five years, before they would actually save it.

There is a common misconception, that if you move to the United States, you have to accept a lower rate of interest. In fact, you can earn exactly the same rate of interest by leaving your GICs and term deposits in Canada, but own them as a non-resident. This may not be the best alternative from an investment strategy or estate planning perspective, but it is possible to have and hold Canadian certificates and bank accounts, while you are a non-resident. See Chapter 6 and 9 for more details on investment strategies to reduce risk, and increase income.

PENSIONS - PARTIALLY TAX FREE

There are some major differences in the way pensions are taxed between the United States and Canada. Revenue Canada taxes all pensions by including 100% of them as taxable income, minus an equivalent exemption of $1,000 each year. The IRS allows pensioners to receive the portion of the pension resulting from the taxpayer's contributions to be tax free. For example, if an individual made 50% of the annual contributions to his or her company pension, they would receive roughly half of their pension upon retirement free from tax. The actual amount received tax free, depends on current interest rates and the life expectancy of the employee, at the time they start receiving their pension.

The IRS considers a pension annuity created from an RRSP, which would be fully taxable in Canada, to be just a regular annuity where only the interest earned each year, is taxable. As a result, a large portion of the monthly payments of your RRSP created pension would be tax free.

Finally, for those Canadians who have had United States employment at some time during their working career and are qualified for U.S. Social Security. The IRS provides for more tax favored treatment, depending on total current income from all sources; anywhere from 100% of U.S. Social Security, to a minimum of 15% can be received free from tax.

Let's look at George again. He is receiving a $50,000 a year pension from his former company that he had contributed to over his 30 years employment. His numbers work out such that the IRS considers 20% of his pension to be excluded from taxation in the United States. Susan did not have a company pension but purchased a 20 year RRSP term annuity from which she receives $20,000 a year. Her return of principal from the annuity, would be approximately $8,500 per year. Figure 8.3 provides the effective results of the tax differential on George and Susan's pensions, by moving to the United States.

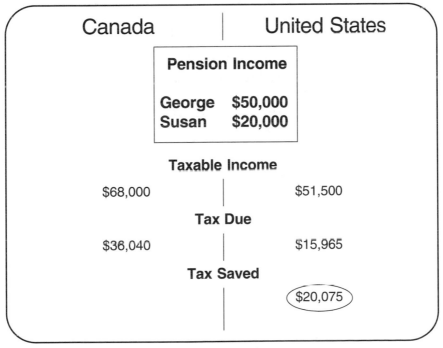

FIGURE 8.3

George and Susan would effectively cut their tax on the pension portion of their income, by 66%. This obviously is a major raise for them, allowing them to keep $54,035 of their pension after tax, instead of only $33,960.

EMPLOYMENT INCOME

Earned income in the United States, is taxed in a similar manner to the same type of income in Canada -- it is added to taxable income. Therefore, earned income is taxed at your marginal tax rates in both countries. This makes a tax comparison between Canada and the United States very simple.

Although Susan is retired from her profession, she still does some management consulting for her former employer, for which she receives a fee of $25,000 a year. Figure 8.4 compares the taxation of this income between the two countries.

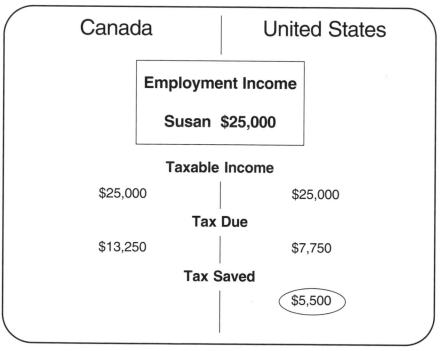

Canada	United States
	Employment Income
	Susan $25,000
	Taxable Income
$25,000	$25,000
	Tax Due
$13,250	$7,750
	Tax Saved
	$5,500

FIGURE 8.4

From Figure 8.4, Susan is provided with a 42% tax reduction and a 47% effective after tax pay raise without even having to talk to her boss. The taxed savings simply results from the fact that the maximum tax rate used is 53% for Ontario and 31% in Florida on this amount of income. Other provincial or state tax comparisons would of course, be different.

CAPITAL GAINS

Capital gains receive some favorable treatment in both Canada and the United States. Once the lifetime $100,000 capital gains exemption in Canada has been used, gains are taxed at a maximum of 40%. In the United States, the maximum federal tax rate on capital gains is 28%. Since there is generally considerable risk in the types of investments that will produce capital gains, most prudent people do not have a large percentage of their assets tied up in this

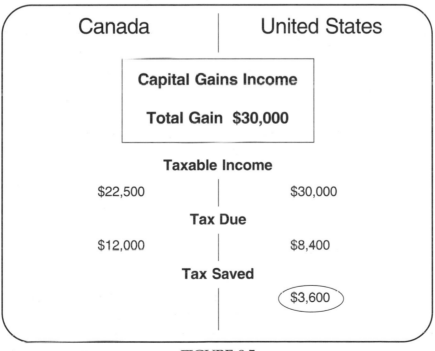

FIGURE 8.5

149

area of investment. Consequently, the tax savings on capital gains is generally, by itself, not enough to create any significant advantages either way when contemplating a move to the United States unless you are a small or closely held business which is highly appreciated (see Chapter 10).

Those who buy and sell real estate for investment purposes, or as their occupation, will find the ability to roll the gain tax free from one property to another in the United States, a great tax savings device in those instances where it is applicable. In addition, there is no deemed disposition tax at death of appreciated assets in the United States as there is in Canada. This means that a surviving spouse, or other beneficiaries who inherit highly appreciated property, can sell it free from capital gains tax.

To site a specific example of a capital gains tax comparison between Canada and the United States, let's turn again to George and Susan who would like to trade in some growth mutual funds, and a bit of real estate. For the current year, they have received capital gains distributions and other trading profits from their mutual funds of $8,000. They also sold a piece of property that netted them a gain of $22,000. They have already used their lifetime Canadian capital gains exemption. Figure 8.5 displays the results.

The Figure 8.5 example, shows a tax reduction on capital gains of over 30% in the United States, even though only 75% of the gain is taxable in Canada. George and Susan have discovered they can get even greater tax savings, in the United States, on their capital gains by using the mutual funds set up as a variable annuity. *These funds provide for the unlimited deferral of capital gains, interest and dividends income until the deferred income is actually withdrawn.*

DIVIDENDS - SMALL SAVINGS

Dividends are taxed very differently in Canada than in the United States. In the U.S. they are taxed the same way as employment income or regular interest, while in Canada dividends are multiplied or grossed up by 125% when calculating taxable income. An offsetting tax credit equal to 13.3% on the federal tax calculation of the grossed up amount is allowed. This makes the maximum tax rate of 35.4% on dividends in Ontario, compared to 31% in Florida.

George and Susan have $10,000 of dividend income. Figure 8.6 compares the net result of being in the maximum tax rates and earning dividends in either country.

Even after considering the Canadian dividend tax credit, George and Susan realize a tax reduction by 12% on their dividends by moving to the United States. As noted in the *Capital Gains* section of this chapter, they can use mutual funds in the form of variable annuities, to defer income tax on dividends in the United States.

In both United States and Canada, dividends are taxed twice, once at the corporate level and again at the individual shareholder's level. So if you owned a dividend paying corporation, both levels of tax must be considered to do a fair comparison between the two countries. For someone with a Canadian controlled small business

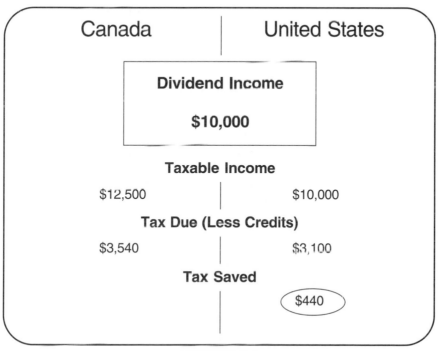

FIGURE 8.6

qualified for the small business tax rate, on income under $200,000 the total tax paid at both the corporate and individual shareholder levels will be less on dividends on the Canadian side of the border. In the United States it is generally better to pay salary and bonuses to owner shareholders than it is to pay a dividend, since salaries are taxed only once at a maximum federal individual rate of 40%.

TOTAL INCOME - THE REAL COMPARISON

The previous examples in this chapter from Figures 8.1 to 8.6 are a good way to compare taxation between Canada and the United States on the major line by line incomes sources. However, this does not in itself provide the complete picture, because it does not take into consideration personal deductions, the progressive tax rates and the different filing options available in the two respective countries. The best way to do a realistic tax comparison, is to take the total world income with deductions, and simultaneously calculate the Canadian and U.S. tax as if the individuals were residents of either country, and then net out the final tax figures.

Since we are already somewhat familiar with George and Susan, we will first do their total tax comparison. George and Susan are both retired, so we will also take a look at Bill and Mary who are medical doctors, still working, with dependent children in college.

George and Susan are both over 65 and own a summer cottage near Ottawa, and a single family dwelling in Naples, Florida. They pay property taxes totaling $6,000 CDN per year, they have no mortgages, they give $5,000 CDN a year to their church, they have two cars and pay $500 CDN per year to license them. They have no sources of income, other than those detailed in Figures 8.1 to 8.6.

George and Susan have cut their tax bill by 54% by moving to the United States and have increased their after tax income by nearly $2,600 per month. *If we were to assume that their joint life expectancy is 20 years and that they could invest this annual tax savings to earn an after tax return of 6%, they would accumulate a total of $1,212,986 in additional net worth over their lifetimes.*

Income

	George	Susan	Combined
CPP	6,500	6,500	13,000
OAS	4,500	4,500	9,000
Pension	50,000	20,000	70,000
Interest	6,750	6,750	13,500
Dividends	5,000	5,000	10,000
Employment	0	25,000	25,000
Capital Gains	15,000	15,000	30,000
Total Income	$87,750	$82,750	$170,500

Canada | United States

Adjustments to Total Income

Canada		United States	
Dividends	+$2,500	Tax Free Interest	-$4,500
Capital Gains	-$7,500	Tax Defer Interest	-$4,500
OAS Repayment	-$8,555	George's Pension	-$10,000
		Susan's Pension	-$8,500
		Pers Exemptions	-$6,267
		Church	-$5,000
		Prop/Veh Taxes	-$6,500
		OAS/CPP	-$11,000

Taxable Income

$156,945 $119,067

Federal Tax Credits

$6775

Net Tax Due

$56,056 $26,948

Tax Savings

$31,108

FIGURE 8.7

153

The tax reduction experienced by George and Susan is quite typical of someone retiring in the United States Sunbelt. Larger savings can be achieved with more comprehensive cross-border financial planning. Those persons whose income comes primarily from RRSP's or RRIF's and other investments, can realize even greater savings than George and Susan did with proper planning.

Now let's take a look at Bill and Mary, in their late forties, who have two children, both in college. Bill is an anesthesiologist earning $200,000 net annually from his practice. Mary is also a doctor who works in a medical clinic as a general practitioner, on a salary of $90,000. They have a large mortgage on their home in Winnipeg with payments of $4,500 per month. They both contribute the maximum to their RRSP's each year. Their property taxes are $5,000 and their two children, age 18 and 19 are still living at home. They have some joint term deposits that earn them about $10,000 per year interest, making their total income $300,000. They have job

Canada		United States	
Adjustments to Total Income of $300,000			
RRSP Contribution	$25,000	Pers Exemption	-$12,533
		AZ State Tax	-$9,385
		Property Taxes	-$5,000
		IRA/SEP Contr	-$43,500
		Mortgage Interest	-$48,000
Taxable Income			
$275,000			$187,946
Federal Tax Credits			
$2,196			
Net Tax Due			
$118,434			$57,750
Tax Savings			
			$60,683

FIGURE 8.8

offers in Arizona, at the same level of income and want to compare their after tax income between Manitoba and Arizona. Figure 8.8 shows the results of that comparison.

Even though their circumstances are quite different, Bill and Mary achieve about the same level of tax reduction, of just under 48%. They would realize an after tax raise in monthly income of over $6,000. This tax savings is due to not only the lower Arizona tax rates, but because they can now deduct their large mortgage interest payments, property tax, state income tax and make a large contribution to their Simplified Employee Pension, rather than an RRSP.

Our two example couples, George and Susan, and Bill and Mary, are both at high income levels. Those who are in lower income brackets will generally experience similar proportionate tax cuts ranging from a 1/3 to 2/3 reduction in overall tax, on the same amount of income. If you are paying less than $10,000 in Canadian

Canadian Non-Resident Withholding Rates

- Interest 15%
- CSB's, Treasury Bonds 0%
- Dividends 15%
- CPP and OAS 0%
- Pensions 15%
- Lump Sum RRSP's 25%
- Rental Income 25%
- Management Fees 15%
- Capital Gains .... Variable%

FIGURE 8.9

taxes, a move to the United States will not likely be of much benefit, unless you have access to low cost medical coverage.

CANADIAN NON-RESIDENT WITHHOLDING TAX

Canadians leaving Canada but still receiving Canadian income, have to look at the Canada — United States Tax Treaty for the rules governing taxation of the income sourced in Canada, while they are a resident of the United States. The treaty, as described in Chapter 1, was created to prevent citizens and residents from being taxed twice on the same income, while at the same time allowing both countries some limited power of taxation according to the income source and type.

A typical example of a situation where the treaty comes into full play, is our George and Susan example in Figures 8.1 to 8.7. They have a number of income sources which they cannot change, their CPP, OAS, and pensions. This means that Revenue Canada, under the tax treaty, will be able to levy some tax on this income as non-residents, since it is sourced in Canada while at the same time, the IRS will have taxation rights on the income, because they are United States residents. The treaty however, ensures that George and Susan will not be double taxed on any of this income, by specifying how the income will be taxed and allowing for tax credits in one country, for taxes paid to the other. The table in Figure 8.9, lists the withholding tax rates between Canada and the United States, on the major forms of income, a Canadian is likely to encounter when moving to the United States.

The rates in Figure 8.9 are withheld at the source, such as at the bank that pays the interest, or the company that pays the pension. *It is the responsibility of the payer to withhold the correct treaty rate from the non-resident's income, and forward that amount to Revenue Canada.* It is the responsibility of the non-resident to notify any applicable payer, that they are, or are becoming residents of the United States. If the improper amount has been withheld, Revenue Canada will send a bill to the non-resident and expect payment. If Revenue Canada cannot find the non-resident, and the payer was at fault for under withholding, they can be held liable for any taxes due.

If the correct non-resident withholding has been taken, the non-resident is not required to file a tax return with Revenue Canada. However, there are special filing options for those non-residents with rental income or pension income if the withholding rate is higher than the actual tax would have been, if that person had been a resident of Canada. For example, if a non-resident has a rental property which earns no net profit, they could elect to file a non-resident return under Section 216 of the Income Tax Act and pay no tax on the gross rental receipts. Similarly, under Section 217 of the Income Tax Act, someone receiving a Canadian pension whose tax rate would have been less than the 15% withholding, had they been a Canadian resident with that pension income only, can file a special return and claim a refund (see restrictions for a Section 217 following later in this chapter in the Withdraw Your RRSP Tax Free section). In addition, they could apply to Revenue Canada for a reduced withholding rate.

Income	George	Susan	W/H Tax
CPP	6,500	6,500	0
OAS	4,500	4,500	0
Pension	50,000	20,000	10,500
Interest	6,750	6,750	0
Dividends	5,000	5,000	1,500
Employment	0	25,000	3,750
Capital Gains	15,000	15,000	10,000
Total Non Resident Withholding Tax			**$25,750**
Total U.S. Tax Due			$26,948
Credit for Cdn W/H Tax			$25,750
Net Tax Payable to U.S.			**$1,198**

FIGURE 8.10

On capital gains income, a non-resident must either face withholding rates of up to 50%, or file for a clearance certificate, prior to the sale of the capital property from Revenue Canada. When Revenue Canada issues the clearance certificate, it will determine what portion of the gain is taxable, and authorize the buyer to withhold at a rate where they are assured of getting all their tax due. The seller must file a Canadian return as a final reconciliation of the transaction, in the year in which the sale occurred.

Payments from RRSP's and RRIF's are considered pension payments subject to the 15% withholding rate as long as they are periodic. Periodic means the RRSP must be in the form of an annuity with payments to at least age ninety. Periodic payments from a RRIF must not exceed twice the annual minimum payment, to qualify for the 15% withholding rate, rather than the lump sum rate of 25%. See the section *Withdraw Your RRSP Tax Free!*

To more clearly illustrate how this system of withholding taxes and credits works, let's look back at George and Susan again, and see what actually happened when they exited Canada for the United States. For this example, we assume that they converted all of their interest bearing bank deposits in Canada to the United States, just as their cross-border financial planner recommended, and that Revenue Canada agreed that a 30% withholding tax on their capital gains was suitable. Refer back to Figure 8.7 if you wish to review George and Susan's income sources and taxes due as Figure 8.10 will only summarize these numbers.

Figure 8.10 indicates that George and Susan would have to pay only $1,198 in taxes to the United States, because the Canadian non- resident withholding tax was allowed as a foreign tax credit on their U.S. return. The credit from the Canadian withholding tax in fact, nearly wiped out any tax they would have had to pay to the IRS, had the income been generated in the United States. You will notice that George and Susan had no withholding on their CPP and OAS, and that the non-resident withholding on their other Canadian income sources was nearly equal to the total United States tax due on their total income. This means they effectively received their CPP and OAS, free from both Canadian and United States taxes.

The foreign tax credit in the United States, is subject to some special rules that can affect the amount of credit actually allowed by the IRS. The example of George and Susan has been simplified somewhat, to show the overall effect of the withholding and credit system under the Canada — United States Tax Treaty. So, on an actual return, their results would likely be slightly different. Had the IRS, under any of its rules, disallowed any of the Canadian tax withheld as a foreign tax credit, it could have been carried forward for up to five years, to be used against future foreign income earned.

WITHDRAW YOUR RRSP TAX FREE!

Many Canadians have small fortunes sitting in their RRSP's, but are very reluctant to withdraw any money from them, because they face such high rates of taxation on the withdrawals. *This section will deal with some of the cross-border financial planning techniques that can help you withdraw even large sums from your RRSP and effectively pay no or very little net taxes.* In many cases, these cross-border financial planning techniques, can provide a major incentive for becoming a United States resident, as the savings, especially on the larger accounts, can be in the thousands of dollars!

The issue of what to do with RRSP's when Canadians exit Canada to take up residency in the United States is more often than not overlooked, especially for those who fail to complete a cross-border financial plan. When taking up residency in the United States, RRSP's can be a great source of tax savings, if they are planned for correctly. Without proper planning, RRSP's can create unnecessary United States taxes, and can potentially be double taxed by both the United States and Canada. Most people either ignore planning for their RRSP's, think there is nothing they need to do, or that they can let their RRSP's sit and accumulate interest, as if they were still a resident of Canada.

How Canadian RRSP's are looked at by the United States Internal Revenue Service, will help explain some of the problems surrounding them, and how we can plan around them. We touched briefly upon this issue earlier in this chapter, in Figure 8.3 with respect to Susan's RRSP annuity pension. *The IRS considers your RRSP to be an ordinary investment looking right through the RRSP trusteeship.* Consequently, whatever the underlying investment is in the RRSP, that is how the IRS will treat it as a resident of the United States. For example, the IRS will consider the contributions you made and the accumulated interest or dividends in a RRSP, as tax paid principal prior to becoming a U.S. resident, but as a resident, will tax interest earned and paid during the year, in the same way as if you had earned the interest in a standard U.S. bank account. Similarly, dividends and capital gains on your RRSP account are subject to U.S. tax, as they are paid or realized, without the deferral of tax provided for by Revenue Canada.

As a U.S. resident, if you were to leave your RRSP's in Canada, the IRS will tax you on all interest, dividends and capital gains earned on your account, even though you may not have actually received them. When you are taxed on income that you do not actually receive, it is called phantom income. Many Canadians with RRSP's, have been in the United States for years, and never realized that they have a United States tax liability on this phantom income. The new Canada — United States Tax Treaty which came into effect in 1985, allows you to make an election annually on your United States return, under Revenue Procedure 89-45, to defer the payment of United States tax on the RRSP phantom income until such time as it was actually withdrawn. Withdrawals of your principal contributions to the RRSP, are not taxed by the Internal Revenue Service at any time.

What then, is the best thing to do with your RRSP's upon leaving Canada? There are no provisions between Canada and the United States for a direct transfer of your RRSP to the U.S. equivalent, an Individual Retirement Account (IRA). Therefore, you have only two options --- withdraw the RRSP's, or make the annual elections under the Treaty to defer U.S. taxation on the income. We recommend the former solution for two key reasons --- the continual exposure to unnecessary tax risk and currency speculation.

If you leave your RRSP in Canada, not only are you subject to the tax rules of both Canada and the United States, but you are subject to any future Canadian tax legislation that could restrict future with-drawals even further than they are now. As recently as December 20, 1991, Revenue Canada made several changes to the Income Tax Conventions Interpretation Act, restricting the definition of what qualifies as a periodic RRIF withdrawal, forcing RRIF holders to pay a 25% withholding rate instead of a 15% rate on withdrawals larger than twice the annual minimum. Expect Revenue Canada to continue to tighten these restrictions, as they are constantly on the look out for more revenue. Just like the old sayings "make hay while the sun shines" or "get out while the getting is good," you can cash in your RRSP's now, and pay as little as zero tax once you leave Canada, so why wait for future legislation to come along that will restrict your options. In addition to these tax risks, persons with estates over $600,000 may face a double taxation in a similar manner to the potential double indemnity on capital gains tax at death discussed in Chapter 4. The double tax arises because Canada will withhold 25% from your RRSP at your death, and this amount will not be allowed as a credit against United States estate tax due.

The second reason to cash in your RRSP's after becoming a United States resident, is to avoid unnecessary currency speculation. We have already covered the hazards unknowingly becoming a currency speculator in Chapter 2. *Keeping an RRSP in Canadian dollars when you are likely to need U.S. dollars for retirement is exposing yourself to unnecessary currency risk.*

Making withdrawals from your RRSP to maximize your bene-fits and minimize your taxes, is no simple task, and should not be done without the supervision of a qualified cross-border financial planner. This is one area of cross-border financial planning where a simple error can be costly and irreversible, so the use of a knowledge-able professional can pay big dividends.

The timing of the withdrawals is critical. You need to match Canadian withholding taxes with U.S. taxability of foreign income. Correct matching of taxes paid to Canada and available foreign tax credits in the United States, can mean the difference between paying 25% or 0% tax on a net basis on your RRSP balance. When calculating the usable foreign tax credits on a U.S. tax return, all sources of foreign income must be considered, not just the RRSP income, along with the non-resident withholding tax on all of them.

For smaller RRSP's, namely those with less than $100,000 in value, staged withdrawals can be controlled to match the foreign tax credits available. Section 217 of the Income Tax Act allows persons who withdraw between $7,000 and $25,000 from their RRSP, and who have no other taxable Canadian income, to file a return, and obtain either a full or partial refund of the withholding tax. Revenue Canada amended Section 217 filing requirements in 1992, eliminating filers who do not derive 50% of their world income from Canada. Consequently, this option is no longer viable for those with substantial U.S. or world income. You need to consider the interest rates on RRSPs, foreign income, amounts withdrawn, and available U.S. tax credits, in order to withdraw your RRSP out of Canada in the shortest time, and at the lowest possible tax rate.

Other than the non-resident withholding tax, you have no further Canadian obligations with respect to your RRSP's, and no need to file a return when making withdrawals, unless you qualify for a refund under Section 217.

TAX ON EXITING CANADA

If you, as a Canadian resident move to the United States, Revenue Canada requires that you file an exit tax return in the year of your departure.

This exit tax return requires regular Canadian tax be paid on all income for the portion of the year up to the departure date along with any capital gains tax due because of the departure. You are deemed to have disposed of certain property on the date of departure. This rule applies to property, such as publicly traded securities and personal property. It does not include taxable Canadian property, such as real estate situated in Canada, or shares of private Canadian corporations. This deemed disposition includes American vacation homes and other similar property. The exit tax return and the deemed disposition tax is due April 30, following the year of departure. You may elect to defer the tax resulting from the deemed disposition if you file Revenue Canada Form T2061 with your tax return, and provide suitable security equal to the amount of deferred tax to Revenue Canada. If you have any of your lifetime capital gains exemption remaining, you may use it for the deemed disposition gain as well.

If you did not sell your Canadian principal residence prior to departing Canada, you need to be aware of some special rules under the Canada — United States Tax Treaty that can help you reduce future capital gains tax on the ultimate sale of the Canadian home while you are a United States resident. In Chapter 3, when we compared the basic differences in taxation between the United States and Canada you saw that Canada does not tax capital gains on the sale of a principal residence while the United States will tax those gains, if they are not rolled over into a new residence of equal or greater value (those over 55 in the United States have up to a $125,000 lifetime exemption). The treaty helps you around this problem by making it appear, for tax purposes, that you purchased the Canadian home at its fair market value the day you entered the United States. As a result, you are responsible to the IRS only for gains on this property from the date you became an official resident. Note that this step up in basis, applies only to your principal residence, no other capital property receives this special treatment. *It is highly recommended that Canadians who keep their principal residence when moving to he United States get a fair market appraisal just prior to leaving Canada and keep it for future tax reference.*

U.S. ESTATE PLANNING

Necessity is the mother of invention. Since there is a greater need for comprehensive estate planning in the United States, there have been many very good and proven techniques developed to help make the management of your estate easier while you are alive, and then provide for a smooth transition to your heirs. Many of these techniques work for Canadians becoming residents of the United States equally as well, and can be used to include assets still remaining in Canada.

When someone is moving or contemplating a move to the United States, cross-border estate planning needs to be a top priority, as there are many complex issues which if not addressed before taking up United States domicile, could cause unnecessary estate settlement costs and death taxes.

Normally the first issue of cross-border estate planning is doing a comparison of what your estate costs and taxes are in Canada, and then in the United States, to see if there is any available advantage in either country. It is not very often in this book that we can state a general rule that applies in almost every case but *couples with estates under $1,600,000 CDN or $1,200,000 US have an unquestionable tax advantage as residents of the United States.* Since there are Spousal Trusts in Canada, and Qualified Domestic-Marital Deduction Trusts in the United States to transfer assets tax free between spouses, we will look at the estate tax and settlement costs at the death of the second spouse, to measure the full impact of these

Assets		Amount Subject to Canadian Death Tax
RRSP/RRIF	$400,000	$400,000
Cdn Residence	$250,000	$0
Mutual Funds	$150,000 (Cost $75,000)	$56,250
U.S. Residence	$250,000 (Cost $100,000)	$112,500*
Land	$150,000 (Cost $50,000)	$75,000
Term Deposit	$100,000	$0
Personal	$80,000	$0
Total	**$1,380,000CDN**	
Canadian Resident Death Taxes		**$412,289**
U.S. Resident Death Taxes		**$0**

* Subject to a U.S. Non Resident Estate Tax in addition to the Canadian Death

FIGURE 8.11

costs and make a proper Canadian — U.S. comparison. Figure 8.11 give us an example of this situation, using a reasonably well off couple with an estate of $1,380,000 CDN, who have both used their lifetime capital gains exemption.

The Canadian death taxes in Figure 8.11, are calculated by taking the amount subject to deemed disposition tax at death of the surviving spouse, and adding in the U.S. non-resident tax on their United States vacation home and the probate fee. The total deemed disposition tax is $341,189, the U.S. non-resident estate tax is $30,400 and the probate fee for an estate of this size in Ontario, would be $20,700. Thus, a total death tax of $412,289 would be payable by this couple's estate if they were Canadian residents at the time of their deaths. If this couple, or at the very least, the surviving spouse, does not undertake some preventive planning, their heirs will pay what amounts to a total of $412,289 Canadian inheritance tax, after the second spouse's death. These taxes will be due right away, within six months of death.

However, if this couple took up residence in the United States, and had a similar asset mix at the time of death, they would have *no estate taxes* due, since the size of their estate would be only $1,033,400 US, less than their total of $1,200,000 US estate tax exemptions. In Chapter 4, we listed some of the double tax consequences of having assets in both Canada and the US, and earlier in this chapter under the heading *Tax on Exiting Canada,* we listed things to look out for when leaving Canada. The complexity of these issues underscores the necessity of consulting with a cross-border financial planner, to ensure you maximize the opportunities and minimize the pitfalls.

For estates over $1,200,000 US per couple, or $600,000 US for individuals, other estate planning techniques can be used to deal economically with almost any estate tax (see the table in Figure 4.2 for the estate tax rates). Substantial United States residents with estates over their personal estate tax exemptions, and who are concerned about their estate depletion as discussed in Chapter 4, will use one or more trusts set aside and funded with income tax savings, to pay any potential estate taxes, even when they total into the millions of dollars. In addition, there are many other effective estate tax planning techniques for larger estates, which go beyond the general scope of this cross-border guide.

Under *The Living Trust - The Simple Solution to the Problems of Wills* section of Chapter 4, we outlined a number of benefits of using a Living Trust in an estate plan. These trusts are used in the United States for estates of any size, to assist in minimizing probate costs and delays. These trusts, combined with wills that are designed to place assets outside trusts into them at death, Powers of Attorney and living wills round off a cross-border estate plan. Powers of Attorney were explained earlier in Chapter 4. A living will is a separate document that deals with the possibility of your becoming incapacitated, connected to life support systems with no hope of recovery. The living will tells your family and medical professionals your wishes, under this set of circumstances.

CROSS-BORDER Q&A

Many of the issues covered in the preceding chapter of this book have already been touched upon in the *Cross Border Q & A* column which appears in *The Sun Times of Canada,* and the author's own newsletter *The Sunbelt Canadian.* A majority of these questions have been posed by readers looking for advice relating to their own specific problems or situations. At the end of this chapter, we have included some typical reader questions, along with our response, to better illustrate and flesh out the concepts presented in the chapter.

Converting E2 Visa Status & Holding Canadian RRSP's

In August of 1990, after obtaining an E2 visa, I moved to the United States and purchased a business and a home. I am a Canadian citizen, residing in the U.S. with my wife and children and would like to establish permanent immigrant status. I own a rental property in Florida under a numbered Ontario corporation. My income is derived from the business in the United States and from dividends received from less than arms length Canadian corporations. As of 1991, I have elected to be taxed in the United States. I still hold an RRSP in Canada and own a private Canadian corporation. I realize these are rather complex issues, but I would like to hear from you.

1. In who's name should any United States assets be held?

2. What should I do with my Canadian assets?

3. What should I do with my Canadian RRSP?

4. What should I do with my United States rental property?

5. Is there anything that can be done to convert my E2 non-immigrant status to immigrant status? My sister is a U.S. resident and holds a Green Card.

— *Larry H., Wilmington, NC*

You are absolutely right! Your questions cover some very complicated issues. Consequently, the answers will also be complex, depending on your ultimate objectives, and other extenuating circumstances.

1. The titling of your United States assets generally would follow the same procedures that you would use in Canada. Business assets would likely best be owned by the business itself, depending on whether you are operating under a sole proprietorship, or are incorporated. Personal assets would be in your and/or your spouse's name. You should also look into using a Family Living Trust with provisions for a Qualified Domestic Trust to own all your assets. This trust would help organize your estate to help avoid probate in Florida, North Carolina and Ontario, and make better use of the United States estate tax exemptions.

2. Unless your Canadian assets are of a nature that there is no comparable asset available in the United States that can produce a similar return on your investment, your life will be greatly simplified if you liquidate all your Canadian assets. Maintaining a Canadian corporation, when your intentions are to permanently reside in the United States, can create double estate tax, subject you to possibly a higher rate of income tax, and force you into special Internal Revenue Service reporting on your Canadian personal holding companies.

3. RRSP's, and what to do with them when you move to the United States will be explained in the next two questions.

4. Your United States rental property in the Ontario company should be moved out of the Ontario company into either your own name, or possibly a United States corporation similar in purpose to the Ontario one. On the United States side of the border, there is no advantage to holding small rental properties in holding companies. In fact, you would likely be at a tax disadvantage by using a United States holding company, not to mention all the extra costs involved with corporations. There are both Canadian and United States tax implications in taking this rental property out of the Ontario corporation, which are too complex to discuss here. I do recommend seeking professional help here, as well as with any other changes you are contemplating, as mistakes can be costly.

5. If your sister has been married to a U.S. citizen and has resided in the United States for more than three years, she can become a United States citizen and sponsor your "Green Card" immigrant status. The waiting time for this type of sibling sponsorship of the "Green Card" is around ten years from application, so you would need to keep renewing your E2 visa until that time. You have some other options to obtaining immigrant status through your company, which may require a somewhat difficult labor certification. A consultation with a good immigration attorney would be advised.

Making RRSP Contributions for the Year Leaving Canada

My husband and I are moving from Toronto, to take up new positions in Florida and will be leaving Canada on what appears to be a permanent basis. Do you have any recommendations as to what to do with our RRSP's before we leave Canada. Is it to our advantage to make RRSP contributions in the year we leave? What will happen once we leave Canada if we keep our RRSP's in Canada? Can they be transferred to a retirement plan in the United States, or should we cash them in before we leave?

— *Lena S., Safety Harbor, FL*

You didn't mention how much, or what types of investments you had in your husband's RRSP's, so I will explore most of the options with you, since this is a very common problem.

First, let's deal with the question of what to do with your RRSP before you leave Canada. Assuming you both have employment income in the same year you are leaving, cashing in your RRSP's will add greatly to your total income for the year, and likely be taxed at your maximum marginal tax rates of 53% in Ontario. Unless you want to lose half of all your accumulated RRSP's savings to Revenue Canada, you should explore other alternatives to cashing them in before you leave Canada.

There are some alternatives which may allow you to withdraw the full balance of your RRSP's at no or very low Canadian taxes.

If your RRSP consists of mutual funds, stocks or other appreciated assets, we recommend you realize these gains prior to becoming a United States resident. You would realize the gains by either liquidating all the investments and transferring the proceeds directly into a new RRSP savings account or short term deposits. If you have mutual funds, this transaction can be accomplished generally at no cost by merely switching from one fund to another, within the same family of mutual funds. This exercise to realize your gains does not effect your Canadian tax one bit, because your investments remain sheltered under your RRSP. However, for American tax purposes, should you liquidate them while a United States resident, you will pay more U.S. tax unless you complete this gain realization process. The United States can tax capital gains on your investments, so by realizing these gains before you take up residency, you are establishing a higher cost basis and hence less United States capital gains, when the investments are eventually sold.

Before you leave Canada, we recommend you make your maximum contribution to your RRSP's for the current year. With Canada's new RRSP rules, which base this year's contributions on last year's income, you can take advantage of some great tax savings. For example, if you and your husband each earned up to $17,500 from your Canadian employment in the current year before you left the country, and could make the maximum RRSP contributions of $12,500 each, based on last year's earnings, you could eliminate any tax on your income in Canada during your year of exit. Your RRSP contributions and your personal credits, would qualify you for a full refund of any tax withheld. At these levels of income, we would estimate a refund of over $8,000 in the short year of your exit.

After taking up residency in the U.S., withdrawals from your RRSP's, if planned correctly can be a great source of tax savings. Without proper planning, they can create unnecessary United States taxes, and could be taxed by both the U.S. and Canada.

There are no provisions between Canada and the United States for a direct transfer of your RRSP to the U.S. equivalent, an Individual Retirement Account (IRA). However, you can cash out of your RRSP's and pay as little as zero taxes, once you leave Canada, and use the net proceeds to contribute your maximum to your IRA's or other tax deductible qualified plans in the U.S.

The background of how Canadian RRSP's are looked at by the United States Internal Revenue Service will help explain the problem and how to plan around it. The Internal Revenue Service (IRS) considers your RRSP to be an ordinary investment, without the deferral of tax that Revenue Canada provides. Consequently, as a U.S. resident, if you were to leave your RRSP's in Canada, the IRS will tax you on all interest, dividends and capital gains on your account, even though you may not have actually received them. When you are taxed on income that you do not actually receive, it is called phantom income. The new Canada —United States Tax Treaty which came into effect in 1985, allows you to make an election annually on your United States return, to defer the payment of United States tax on the RRSP phantom income, until it is actually withdrawn. Withdrawals of your principal contributions to the RRSP, are not taxed by the Internal Revenue Service, at anytime.

Revenue Canada will tax all lump sum RRSP withdrawals by non-residents at a flat 25% withholding rate, and periodic withdrawals at a 15% rate. On December 20, 1991, Revenue Canada made several changes to the Income Tax Conventions Interpretation Act restricting the definition of what qualifies as a periodic RRSP withdrawal, forcing planners to use some alternate methods to qualify clients for the 15% withholding rate instead of the 25% rate.

The question of what to do now, should be somewhat easier to explain, now that you have some background. Since Revenue Canada has made it next to impossible for younger RRSP holders to have their withdrawals classified as periodic payment, a series of lump sum withdrawals at the 25% withholding rate is probably the best alternative. If you arrange for a series of annual lump sum withdrawals, and the total of these withdrawals is less than $7,000, you can file, as a non-resident, under Section 217 of the Canada Income Tax Act, to get a full refund of the withholding tax each year. If the payouts are more than $7,000 but less than $25,000, you could receive a partial refund of the withholding tax under Section 217.

Other than the withholding tax, you have no further Canadian obligations with respect to your RRSP's. However, you are going to have to reconcile the income earned on this RRSP, with the Internal Revenue Service, by adding it to your U.S. taxable income. You will receive foreign tax credits for the tax withheld by Canada on your United States return. There are a number of alternatives to consider when reporting the income on your United States return, but without knowing your United States tax information, it is difficult to speculate which alternative will be best. You will likely need some professional help in this area.

Moving Back To Canada

Relocation between Canada and the U.S. is not just a one way street to the South. There are also a lot of Canadians who return to Canada after years of living and working in Florida as U.S. residents. These people would love to hear something about their tax planning opportunities as well, such as Deferred U.S. Annuities.

Florida tax planners are in general, not really knowledgeable about Canadian tax law and changes in the past.

— *Lamont S., Naples, FL*

Great question. It is true that movement between Canada and the U.S., is not a one way street. We often deal with Canadians and Americans moving back and forth in both directions.

Since we live in such a ever-changing society, good cross-border planning will generally keep all doors open so persons moving out of Canada may move back without adverse tax or other consequences.

Tax planning opportunities and concerns arising when moving from the U.S. back to Canada are numerous, and not necessarily the reversal of the planning procedure of the original move to the U.S.

Unrealized gains on stocks, bonds and investment real estate are best realized prior to exiting the U.S. for Canada. The maximum capital gains rate in most provinces is 37% whereas the U.S. maximum is now 28%. If you had never used your lifetime $100,000 Canadian Capital Gain, prior to moving to the U.S., you will requalify to use it, once you take residence and start filing tax returns again in Canada.

If you have a large capital gain built up in the personal residence you own in the U.S., you should take advantage of the lifetime $125,000 tax exemption, by selling the residence prior to leaving the U.S., or you could lose it. Canada will not recognize this U.S. lifetime exemption, nor will the U.S. recognize the Canadian principal residence capital gain exemption.

If you have acquired IRA's in the U.S., which are equivalent to Canada RRSP's, you may get some good tax breaks when you head back to Canada. Canada will tax you only on the interest and dividends you earn on these accounts, once you become a resident, and not on the principal and interest accumulated prior to leaving the U.S. Consequently, once you have exited the U.S. and providing you are over 59 1/2, you may withdraw the IRA's at no or very low tax rates, depending on your other sources of U.S. Income.

If you own deferred annuities of any type when you move back to Canada, they will lose their ability to shelter income build up from current Canadian taxation. Canada requires you to report all interest, dividend and realized capital gains on deferred annuities on a current basis, and will not allow you to accrue this income, to defer the payment of tax. Annuities are best cashed in, and invested in term deposits or similar Canadian investments, or converted to annuity payout options.

If you are collecting U.S. Social Security, under the Canada — United States Tax Treaty, you will be allowed to exclude 50% of this income from Canadian taxation. If you are a U.S. Green Card holder when you take up permanent residency back in Canada, you will be required to surrender it. If you don't, not only are you going against U.S. Immigration regulations but the Internal Revenue Service will continue to tax you as a resident. If you have become a U.S. citizen or a dual Canadian/U.S. citizen, much of what I have indicated here as planning opportunities, will apply differently to you, unless you directly and formally surrender your U.S. citizenship. If you are a dual citizen, and are a resident of Canada, you will need to be filing full returns in both Canada and the U.S. on your world income and taking allowable credits back and forth to avoid being double taxed on that income.

When you re-enter Canada, be prepared for a tax shocker. There is no tax free or tax deferred income available in Canada. There are fewer deductions and the marginal tax rates are much higher. If your primary sources of income are interest and pensions, you can expect your income tax bill to nearly double. You will of course, be the beneficiary of Canada's comprehensive medical care system and more highly developed social welfare systems. So what you give up in taxes, you may well recover in security.

In any case, when you are moving cross-border in either direction, you need a detailed plan with the assistance of a professional, fully knowledgeable on both sides of the border, to direct you through the maze of opportunities and pitfalls.

CHAPTER NINE

GIVE MY REGARDS
TO WALL STREET

INVESTING AS A
U.S. RESIDENT

A sound investment strategy should be built around the basic concepts of asset allocation, risk allocation, risk control and performance tracking. Risk control and performance tracking are easily understood. Attention to asset allocation is necessary due to the cyclical nature of our economy. The country's economy changes from periods of prosperity and low interest rates, to times of recession and high rates. Proper asset allocation strategies allow portfolios to contain different types of investments that will perform well in various economic environments. So regardless of which way the economy in the United States or Canada is heading, you have a relatively steady return with good safety of principal.

In Chapter 6 we spoke a great deal about investment types, investment risk, and currency fluctuations mainly from the perspective of the non-resident Canadian. A Canadian taking up residency in the United States, also needs to consider all these factors, make some necessary adjustments and position their investments in such a way that the proper balance between assets is achieved to realize their financial goals. For most people this is a difficult task, because not only are they treading new ground in the United States, but there are interlocking factors that need to be addressed simultaneously among the financial planning areas of taxation, estate, cash flow and investments. In other words, changes in one segment of your financial plan, may require modification to several other areas as well. There are also cross-border considerations, since most Canadians moving to the United States leave several investments in Canada. These investments need to be integrated with their United States investment program in order to derive maximum benefit.

The first step is determining what your actual objectives and needs are, from your investment portfolio. This may be restating the obvious, but our experience in financial planning has proven that many people neglect doing even a basic analysis of what exactly they want or need from their investment portfolio. Consequently, their current investments do not often match their needs. Figure 9.1 is a quick exercise designed to help you determine your priorities.

Investment Priority Checklist

Inflation ☐

Tax Advantages ☐

Safety ☐

Diversification ☐

Professional Management ☐

Growth ☐

Liquidity ☐

Income Now ☐

Income Later ☐

FIGURE 9.1

The investment characteristics listed in Figure 9.1, are the main attributes one should consider when looking at investments. In the boxes on the right, prioritize these characteristics by assigning a numerical value from 1 to 9; one being the most important to you, and nine the least. Use the same number only once, so when you are finished, you will have a list of the nine main characteristics, in order of their importance. Now you will have a guide from which you can measure how well your investments meet your priorities. For example, if liquidity and inflation protection are the two most important characteristics, and you have most of your money locked into term deposits or GIC's of one form or another, your investments are mismatched to your own needs, since neither of those investments will provide inflation protection or liquidity.

There are some sophisticated computerized asset allocation programs used by professional money managers, which can compare your current portfolio with twenty or more years of historical data, to determine the overall level of risk or variability your investments have, and the expected rate of return, assuming you leave the investments as they are. These programs, can also recommend changes or "optimize" a portfolio, to achieve greater returns at reduced levels of risk. Historical data cannot guarantee future results, but this sort of analysis is very useful in quantifying levels of risk, determining the relationship of one investment to another, and looking at how changes to an individual portfolio can affect the risk and return parameters. When setting up your United States investment program, this type of analysis should be routine, and can provide you with greater security, and increased return.

The next step in developing your portfolio, is to determine your overall objectives. There are four key objectives or modes, that can be realistically achieved by an investment portfolio:

- **Income**

Who Should Consider this Objective:

- Investors whose primary concern is current income.
- Investors who will tolerate only minor erosions of principal in any given year.

- Investors who are not concerned with the long term effects of inflation on their purchasing power.

Typical Investors

- Retired individuals looking to enhance their income in order to live more comfortably.

- Conservative investors willing to accept a relatively small degree of principal fluctuation.

- Families who need to supplement their income.

Objective

The Income and Preservation of Principal objective seeks a high level of current income with liquidity and relatively low annual principal fluctuation. This objective does not seek to maintain purchasing power against inflation.

Management Technique

Use mutual funds that invest in U.S. or foreign government securities, investment grade corporate debt securities, high quality mortgage securities, investment grade and/or insured municipal bonds. Equity exposure is limited to 30% of the total portfolio.

- **Growth And Income**

Who Should Consider this Objective:

- Investors with long investment horizons (3+ years).

- Investors who want some long-term growth along with stability of principal.

- Investors who want current income that could increase each year to offset inflation.

- Investors who can live with the possibility of some losses as well as gains in any given year.

Typical Investors

- Retired individuals concerned about the effects of inflation on their retirement income.

- Conservative working individuals looking to build a nest-egg.

Objective

The Income With Growth objective seeks to provide an income stream that on the average, increases annually to compensate for the loss of purchasing power, due to rising inflation. This objective also strives to maintain portfolio purchasing power. This objective will entail some year to year volatility in portfolio values.

Management Technique

Use mutual funds that invest in large capitalization stocks and investment grade debt securities. Investments in cash/short-term debt and fixed income funds will comprise at least 20% of the portfolio for each category. Thus, maximum exposure to equity markets will be 60%.

- **Growth**

Who Should Consider this Objective:

- Investors with long-term investment horizons (5+ years).

- Investors who can live with the possibility of large losses as well as gains in any given year.

- Investors who do not have to live on all of the income generated from their investments.

Typical Investors

- Working individuals who are looking to aggressively build an asset base.

- Retired individuals who at present require little or no investment income to live on.

- Bank savers who realize that by keeping their investments solely in bank accounts they may be sacrificing opportunities for superior long-term investment returns.

Objective

The Growth objective is to seek capital appreciation over the long run (3-10 years). Current income is not a consideration.

Management Technique

Use mutual funds that will not be limited by size or type of company. Investments in cash and fixed income funds will usually be minimal, but must comprise at least 10% of the portfolio. Thus, maximum exposure to equity markets will be 90%.

• Aggressive Growth

Who Should Consider this Objective

- Investors with long-term investment horizons (3-10 years).
- Investors who want a chance to maximize long-term growth.
- Investors who can tolerate potentially large year to year volatility in the value of their investment.

Typical Investors

- Aggressive retirees not needing investment income to live on.
- Aggressive middle-aged investors lolling to build a retirement nest egg.
- Young investors not "now" oriented.

Objective

The Aggressive Growth strategy offers a potentially high long-term returns (5-10 years) at the cost of year to year volatility. This offers the highest potential for growth over the long run, but will probably be the most volatile of all the objective in any given year.

Management Technique

Use mutual funds that will not be limited by size or type of company. Investments in cash and fixed income funds will usually be minimal. Equity exposure can range as high as 100%. It is anticipated that his objective will make use of small company funds in both developed countries and emerging markets to a greater degree than the Growth objective.

Once you have determined your own objectives, you are nearly 90% complete in developing your investment portfolio. The final 10% is important --- the actual investment selection. A professional money manager can select and maintain the investments that match your objectives, making future modifications as your objectives change. Refer back to the section in Chapter 6 titled *Choosing an International Investment Manager,* which will assist in locating the best management firm to meet your needs.

The U.S. provides a wide variety of investments to achieve any investment objective, many of which are tax advantaged. These investments allow investors to achieve greater tax savings without sacrificing liquidity, diversification or increased risk.

PENSIONS AND SOCIAL BENEFITS

Whether you are retired or not, a major objective in cross-border financial planning, is to position yourself to qualify for both Canadian and U.S. government social programs; CPP and OAS in Canada and Social Security in the United States. To qualify for these benefits requires careful long term planning. Canada Pension Plan benefits are earned by being employed in Canada for ten years or longer. Once you have exited Canada, the benefit goes with you. You can apply at age sixty or wait longer, in order to qualify for increased benefits. But the longer you wait, the more zero income years you will have reducing your average monthly earnings, offsetting potential increases by delaying the payment of benefits. Widows can qualify for a reduced benefit based on their spouses earnings record.

To qualify for full Old Age Security benefits, you need to be a resident of Canada for forty years past the age of 18. Anything less will result in a proportionate reduction in benefits. For example, if you had only thirty years in Canada past age 18 you would receive 75% of the maximum monthly benefit.

Those receiving CPP and OAS may recall from Chapter 8 under the section headed *Get 50% of Your CPP Tax Free and Avoid the OAS Clawback,* that there are great tax savings while receiving these benefits while a resident of the United States.

Before we explain how to qualify for U.S. Social Security, we want to make you aware of another, sometimes very beneficial, treaty between Canada and the U.S., the Canada — United States Social Security Agreement. This provides for a coordination of benefits between the two countries, so that citizens spending time in both countries are not disadvantaged by any loss of benefits.

As a result, a Canadian moving to the United States can qualify for a U.S. monthly benefit as early as age 62, by working as little as 18 months and earning as little as $200 per month. The normal qualifying time is ten years of earnings. *With United States Social Security, the spouse of the qualifying person also automatically qualifies to receive approximately 50% of the amount of the spouse, even though they may have never contributed to the system.* A Canadian who marries a United States resident who is receiving or who qualifies for Social Security from their U.S. employment can, after one year of marriage, receive 50% of their spouses monthly amount for life indexed for inflation. The universal coverage plan currently being debated is expected to dramatically change the U.S. health care system. The impact of these proposed changes may take many years to materialize, but the ultimate goal is to improve access to health coverage for all legal residents and citizens of the U.S.

Even retired Canadians who become U.S. residents at age 70 or less, should attempt to put in the minimum amount of qualifying time for Social Security and Medicare. This can be accomplished by earning about $2,500 a year, working part-time, doing some consulting work, or by holding a seat on a board of directors. You need 18 months of work to qualify for benefits, and up to 120 months to qualify for free United States Medicare as well. Canadians often tend to downplay the fact that they've worked in the United States, or for an American company. If you worked in the U.S. anytime after 1933 when Social Security began, you will have accumulated useful quarters towards a monthly benefit or Medicare.

United States Social Security benefits are entirely tax free for a married couple with less than $40,000 total income, and after that up to 85% of it must be included in taxable income.

Canadians who have made contributions to a company pension plan, will be able to claim a portion of their pension as tax free return of principal, while a resident in the United States. The exact amount of tax free pension is determined by using the size of the pension annuity purchased, your age and the IRS tables.

U.S. MEDICAL COVERAGE

Canadians routinely hear about Americans being denied medical treatment because they have no money or insurance. Americans hear about the evils of Canada's *socialist* medical system; patients dying from inadequate care or long waiting lists for surgery. In reality, things are seldom as grim as the media portrays them, and these horror stories have been fabricated by special interest groups, and advocates of one particular system. The most important thing to remember about the U.S. medical system is that it is not inherently more or less humane than the Canadian system; it is just different.

American hospitals and health care providers usually operate on a profit making basis. They compete for patients and this competition results in improved access to more sophisticated medical technology. This abundance of medical resources means that a medium-sized American city may have more specialized diagnostic equipment such MRI scanners, than in all of Canada. The down-side of the equation, is that patients under 65 must either pay for the services out of their own pockets, or buy health insurance to cover medical expenses. Those without either, generally have access to free medical care through a system of county hospitals, which operate in much the same way as Canadian hospitals. Available U.S. medical care can vary greatly from state to state, just like in Canada, where there are numerous inter-provincial differences in applying federal medicare guidelines.

For a new Canadian resident to the United States, we recommend you purchase private health insurance. For those under age 65 with no pre-existing conditions, there are many insurance companies that will provide coverage at reasonable cost. The cost of coverage varies from state to state, with California and Florida tending to be more expensive. The best value by far, is what is known as catastrophic coverage --- insurance that only pays when a claim exceeds a specified dollar amount like $2,500, $5,000, $10,000 or even $25,000. This type of coverage can cost from $50 to $200 per month, depending on your age and the deductible level chosen.

Some Canadian retirees may find their pension plans, will provide full or partial U.S. coverage. Retired federal government employees are eligible through their group plan, called GMSIP, for supplemental coverages, that will pay all reasonable doctor and prescription drug costs as well as a small amount toward daily hospital expenses in the United States.

For those over age 65, the choices are more limited, since most Americans at that age go onto U.S. Medicare. Because of this, there is little demand for individual plans other than Medicare supplements. Consequently, the key cross-border financial planning strategy is to ensure the Canadian resident of the United States, becomes eligible for American Medicare. Figure 9.3 outlines the key means to qualify for U.S. Medicare.

There are insurers who will provide supplements to fill in gaps left by Medicare coverage. These medigap policies currently cost up to about $75 a month, depending on the level and type of medigap

U.S. Medicare Eligibility

- Age 65 or older, and one or more of the following:

- Five years or more as a legal U.S. resident or Green Card holder; or

- U.S. Citizen (including derivative citizen); or

- Married to a U.S. citizen or resident on Social Security who qualified through their own employment.

FIGURE 9.3

chosen. Canadians who have not contributed the minimum forty quarters (120 months) to U.S. Social Security through employment, or who are not married to a U.S. resident or citizen who has made the necessary contributions, can expect to pay around $300 per month for U.S. Medicare coverage.

For those Canadians over 65 who do not yet meet the five year residency requirement for Medicare, there are few options. Chapter 5 referred to one insurance product, Nomad Travel Insurance's Plan II, that provides some coverage to Canadians who are not on provincial medicare. Premiums run around $150 per month for up to $100,000 in coverage. Another solution is to self-insure by setting aside all, or a portion of the annual tax savings into a highly liquid investment account. In Chapter 8, Figure 8.7, our couple saved nearly $30,000 a year in taxes. If they set aside these tax savings in a money market account, they would build a self insurance fund sufficient to cover most major hospital stays, within a few years.

U.S. health insurance and Medicare does not cover extended care in nursing homes or similar facilities, therefore a separate policy to cover these expenses is required. A large number of insurance companies offer this coverage, but great caution is advised. Premiums can vary as much as 200% to 300%, for the identical coverage. The minimum recommended coverage is $100 per day for up to four years with an inflation rider. Premiums from a good A⁺ rated insurance company can range between $50 to $200 per month, depending on your age at the time the policy is taken out. This coverage can be applied for at any time, beginning at about age 50.

Insurance premiums paid for any of the medical coverages referred to in this section are deductible, as an itemized medical expense on your U.S. tax return. However, total monthly premiums can be substantial, especially for those who do not qualify for free U.S. Medicare. This added cost, has to be weighed against the potential income tax and other savings of becoming a United States resident. In George and Susan's example in Chapter 8, they are able to save enough in taxes just from their CPP and OAS clawback, to pay for good medical insurance coverage in the United States.

TAKING CARE OF
BUSINESS

HOW SMALL BUSINESS OWNERS
CAN REAP HUGE REWARDS

T here is no other area of cross-border financial planning that offers the owners of small, closely-held businesses more income tax saving potential than moving to the U.S. Consequently, a good cross-border financial plan can save a business owner between several thousand to several millions of dollars, depending on the size or the nature of the business. Most of these planning opportunities arise solely because a cross-border move is contemplated and would not be available to the business owner if they were not in the process of moving.

The major considerations that small business owners need to be aware are outlined in the next five sections.

A CANADIAN CORPORATION CAN ASSIST WITH U.S. IMMIGRATION

Many a successful entrepreneur has worked hard establishing their business may later want to retire, or just sell the business and try something new. He then applies the same amount of diligence to selling the business, and when the money from the sale is sitting in the bank, and all the income taxes are paid, he starts thinking about retiring to the American Sunbelt. Unfortunately, our hypothetical business owner may have just sold off his simplest and best means of U.S. immigration. As you may recall, the U.S. immigration procedures outlined in Chapter 7, all require some form of business or a family connection for U.S. Immigration. So, if there are no close family members in the U.S. or you have sold your principal business, you may need to establish a new business, in order to complete your immigration. A better route for business owners would be to complete a cross-border plan before the sale of the business has been completed. A sale could either be delayed for a short period of time, or structured in such a way to incorporate the necessary means to acquire a Visa or Green Card. This forward planning could save the business owner a great deal of time and money. In addition, the failure to complete a cross-border plan before a business is sold, could mean that the vendor may have paid a great deal more income tax on the sale than necessary, as outlined in the next section of this chapter.

HOW TO TAKE A CAPITAL GAINS TAX HOLIDAY

Canadian small business owners are currently limited to a once in a lifetime tax free capital gains exemption of $500,000. If the proper planning has been undertaken, then this exemption may be effectively doubled by including a spouse as a co-owner of the business(es). What happens if you have no exemption remaining, or your capital gains exceed the $500,000 or $1,000,000 limitations? A tax rate, which is currently 40% in most provinces, is applied to the amount of capital gains not eligible for the exemption. So how much can you save doing it the other way? A properly drafted cross-border financial plan, can reduce this tax liability to just 15%, using certain provisions included in the Canada-U.S. Tax Treaty. The 15% tax can then be recovered in the U.S. through foreign tax credits on income generated by a properly designed investment portfolio. The net result is that a successful business owner can sell their business and effectively pay no net tax. This no net tax scenario can apply even if the proceeds from the business are $500,000, $5,000,000, or more!

The means to accomplish these potentially enormous tax savings are based on sound legal precedents, but are much too complex to even attempt to explain within the context of a general guide such as this book. The key point that business owners should be aware of, is that these tax savings are possible and available to you. To use them to their maximum advantage, you need to seek the services of a qualified cross-border financial planing specialist, early in the selling process.

TAX RAMIFICATIONS OF MAINTAINING A CANADIAN CORPORATION

If a Canadian business owner wishes to maintain a Canadian corporation after becoming a resident of the U.S., they must deal with a number of issues. First of all, unless an election is made to go through a deemed disposition of the corporate shares on exit from Canada, there is no exit or deemed disposition tax on the shares. Consequently, the sale of the corporate shares after becoming a U.S. resident, may be subject to both Canadian and U.S. capital gains tax, as calculated by the increase in share value since their original acquisition, or creation of the corporation. The Canada - U.S. Tax Treaty does however, make some provision for sufficient tax credits to prevent outright double taxation on this gain. If the owner were to die in the U.S, they may still be subject to the double Estate Tax, a syndrome outlined in Chapter 4. Proper planning can help eliminate or at least greatly reduce any capital gains tax or estate due on the sale or wind up of a business, or the death of the business owner. Another issue that a Canadian business owner living in the U.S. needs to address, is that if the Canadian company is largely a passive one earning income from rentals and investments, it will likely be considered a Foreign Personal Holding Company by the IRS and be subject to a myriad of reporting and other requirements. For example, if the company's fiscal year is not Dec. 31, calendar year reporting of the corporate income must be provided, and tax paid as if the shareholder(s) personally owned the corporate assets. This tax must be paid whether or not it is actually distributed to the shareholders during that year. Considering all of the IRS reporting requirements on Foreign Holding Companies, there is little or no advantage to maintaining a Canadian company of this type. Canadian companies reporting active business income are not subject to any special rules on reporting income, if the owner is a U.S. resident. The owner is only taxed on the income from the holding company in the same year that the IRS will tax you on it. With an active Canadian company, and to a lesser extent a holding company, one very good method to reduce corporate income from the operation is to collect a reasonable management fee. The Canadian corporation would be able to deduct the management fee in full, and under the Canada - U.S. Tax Treaty, management fees are only subject to a flat 15% withholding tax. The 15% withholding tax is fully recoverable in the U.S., through the Foreign Tax credit. If the actual management work is done on the U.S. side of the border, then the Canadian company can pay a reasonable management fee to the owner, or to a related U.S. company exempt from Canadian withholding. The net result, is that income can be removed from the Canadian company without Canadian tax and taxed at the lower U.S. rates. The final tax rate paid will be determined by the owners marginal tax rate and his state of resident in the U.S. If Canadian salaries are taken by U.S. resident shareholders, then the shareholders would have to file non-resident Canadian returns and pay tax on the Canadian salary. The Canada - U.S. Tax Treaty states that if the salary remains under $10,000 no Canadian return need be filed.

What are the estate planning considerations of a Canadian corporation owned by a U.S. resident? As we have seen in Chapter 8, U.S. residents are taxed at death, on their world-wide assets. A Canadian who becomes a resident of the U.S. without proper planning, could subject all his Canadian holdings to the U.S. estate tax. In addition, he may face double taxation from the Canadian deemed disposition tax at death. A proper cross-border plan would use one or more living and/or spousal trusts, to eliminate or greatly reduce both levels of tax by either Canada and the United States. Again, this kind of planning needs to be completed prior to a business owner immigrating to the U.S. Once, you become a U.S. resident, the number of planning choices for a business owner to avoid unnecessary estate taxes, is significantly reduced.

CHAPTER ELEVEN

IN GOD
WE TRUST

CHOOSING A CROSS-BORDER
PLANNING PROFESSIONAL

I ndividuals in Canada, or the United States with financial interests in only the country where they reside, face a single set of
rules, making it relatively easy to obtain the services of a
competent financial planner, accountant or lawyer who can provide
the necessary expertise and advice when required. However, as soon
as a Canadian begins spending time or purchases real estate, or a
business in the United States, there are two new sets of tax rules, the
Canada — United States Tax Treaty, and the Internal Revenue
Code, that need to be considered, as well as numerous other cross-
border financial issues that must dealt with. These rules and
considerations are complex, and are often in conflict with one
another. Even a knowledgeable individual may have difficulty
grasping all the implications, and potentially costly mistakes are
easily made. To make things more difficult, cross-border rules are so
complex and highly specialized, that adequate professional advice is
not easy to find. It can be an arduous job for most professionals, just
learning and keeping current with a single country's rules, let alone
make the time and effort to learn both Canadian and U.S. rules.

Consequently, there are few professionals who have undertaken the task of becoming proficient in both American and Canadian immigration, financial and estate planning matters.

THE TEAM APPROACH

Any Canadian with assets in the United States, and certainly anyone who moves to the United States, will require the assistance of one or more professionals from either Canada or the United States. Because there are so many separate areas of expertise required to complete a valid cross-border financial plan, no one professional can successfully cover all areas of implementation. Consequently, our recommendation is that you opt for a team approach to cross-border financial planning.

The cross-border financial planning team may consist of two or more professionals from either country, depending on the complexity

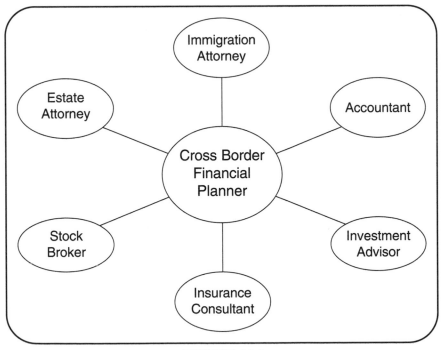

FIGURE 11.1

of your situation. Picking the right members of your team is critical and should be done in a similar manner to choosing a doctor or medical team. You would go first to a general practitioner or family doctor, who would assess your total health, provide the treatment that is within his scope of care, and then recommend or refer you to a specialist. The general practitioner monitors and coordinates all the other medical services, to ensure that treatments are not being duplicated, or conflicting with one another, and they are all focusing on the same objective. Once your medical condition has been treated, the general practitioner will probably monitor your condition, to watch out for any future complications.

Your first step then, in prudent cross-border financial planning, should be to find a good general practitioner. The cross-border financial planner can draw up a written cross-border plan for you, refer you to the individual experts you may require, and then implement the plan by acting as your team leader. Your planner can coordinate other team members to complete your plan in a timely and effective manner. Figure 11.1 displays one possible organizational chart for a typical cross-border financial planning team.

Not everyone is going to need all the advisors listed in Figure 11.1. Some may require more or less. For example, a winter visitor may only require a cross-border financial planner to find a U.S. estate attorney or provide investment advice for their assets, while someone moving to the United States, might require the assistance of both a Canadian and an American accountant, in addition to all the other advisors. Even though Figure 11.1 indicates separate advisors for six different services, several of them may be obtained from the same person or firm. For example, an experienced cross-border financial planner, would likely have the necessary level of expertise in the areas of investment, tax and insurance, to eliminate the need for separate advisors in these areas.

LOCATING A GOOD CROSS-BORDER PROFESSIONAL

For those moving to the United States, it may be best to choose your financial planning team on the U.S. side of the border, particularly the cross-border financial planner who is your team leader.

191

Once you have a team leader in place, they should be given the names of all your existing advisors, so they can assess the situation, and determine what other team members, if any, are required.

The best way to find the right cross-border financial planner to lead your team, is by referral. If you have a friend or relative, or know of someone who has used a cross-border financial planner in a similar situation, ask them for a referral. If not, check with professional organizations such as the Canadian Association of Financial Planners (CAFP), in Toronto, or the Institute for Certified Financial Planners (ICFP), in Denver. These are the key professional associations that educate and license financial planning professionals in Canada and the United States. CAFP has local chapters in most major Canadian cities, and the ICFP in major American cities. They can be located by using the business listings in the telephone book.

The CAFP in Canada controls the use of Chartered Financial Planner (CFP) and Registered Financial Planner (RFP) professional designations in Canada. They are responsible for establishing standards, and conducting courses and examinations for individuals wishing to make financial planning their career. To become an RFP, one must first pass the three year, six course CFP program, or an equivalent professional program, have at least two years experience in financial planning, write a very comprehensive examination, and be an active member of the CAFP. To maintain full membership in CAFP, the Registered Financial Planner must meet continuing educational requirements, have errors and omissions insurance, follow the association's code of ethics, and pay membership dues. We recommend that any Canadian planner you engage have a minimum RFP designation.

The ICFP in the United States, works closely with the College for Financial Planning in Denver, establishing standards and requirements for those wishing to become Certified Financial Planners (CFP). Once the CFP educational and experience requirements have been met, there is a separate board, the IBCFP, that licenses individuals to use and maintain the CFP designation in the United States. A Canadian CFP cannot use their Canadian CFP designation in the United States, unless they have spent another two or three years completing the educational and licensing standards of the IBCFP. The College for Financial Planning has also developed a post graduate Masters of Science degree, in Financial Planning, for those who wish to further their studies in the United States. We recommend that any planner you engage in the United States have a CFP designation, and preferably hold a Masters Degree in Financial Planning, or possess the equivalent experience.

The cross-border financial planner selected to be your team leader should have a minimum RFP designation in Canada, or a CFP in the United States. Although rare, the ideal cross-border financial planner would have both a Canadian RFP and an American CFP, with financial planning experience in both countries.

When interviewing a prospective cross-border financial planner, do not hesitate to ask for references of other Canadians for whom they have successfully completed a cross-border financial plan, or developed a United States non-resident estate plan. Figure

Choosing a Cross Border Financial Planner

Designations Held:
CFP (Canada) ☐
CFP (U.S.) ☐
RFP (Canada) ☐
Other ☐

Education:
Degrees ☐
Post Grad. ☐
Other ☐

Experience: ___ yrs Canada; ___ yrs U.S.

Professional Association Member:
CAFP ☐
ICFP ☐
Other ☐

Can Provide References: Yes ☐ No ☐

Provides Written Fee Agreement: Yes ☐ No ☐

FIGURE 11.2

11.2 provides a summary checklist to use, when you are interviewing potential candidates.

WHAT ABOUT USING AN ACCOUNTANT?

Many people are under the assumption that Charted Accountants (CA) in Canada, and Certified Public Accountants (CPA) in the United States, are qualified to do financial planning, whether it be for a cross-border situation or not. While CA's and CPA's are skilled in preparing financial statements, and are generally qualified to give tax advice in their own country, problems arise when it comes to investment selection, insurance counselling and estate planning. Professional accountants, by training and temperament are neither investment counselors, or estate planners, nor do they generally have a good working knowledge of insurance matters.

Consequently, qualified, professional accountants make excellent cross-border financial planning team members, but because of their narrow focus, are not always suitable as team leaders, particularly in the area of plan implementation.

WHAT TO EXPECT FROM CROSS-BORDER FINANCIAL PLANNERS

Many people have never heard of cross-border financial planning. As a result, they have no solid concept of what it entails or what they should expect. By reading this far in this book, you should now have a pretty good grasp of the number and complexity of problems you'll encounter preparing any good cross-border financial plan. The sheer number of possibilities can be overwhelming.

A professional cross-border financial planner can very quickly sort through this myriad of rules and regulations, and very expeditiously tell you which rules apply to your situation, and how to incorporate them into your planning objectives. Expect a written plan which will address all of your concerns, along with a detailed analysis with specific recommendations. For a Canadian moving to the United States, the cross-border plan should:

- Tell you how each of your assets will be taxed by either country before and after exiting Canada.

- Provide a Canadian and United States net worth and cash flow statement.

- It should provide detailed tax projections on all the tax options available to you.

- Provide a risk management plan to safeguard you from any financial disasters in medical or liability expenses.

- Provide a complete cross-border estate plan, that looks after all your assets, whether they are located in Canada or the United States, and takes into account who your beneficiaries are, where they are located, and what are your personal desires.

- Provide a complete investment program taking into consideration your income needs, your tax bracket, your risk tolerance, the location and liquidity of your assets, and the size of your estate.

- Provide a retirement and benefit plan to maximize CPP, OAS and Social Security benefits, and ensure your income and assets are not depleted during you and your spouse's lifetimes.

Clear and easy to understand verbal and written communications are imperative from any cross-border financial planner you choose. Nothing is more frustrating, than hiring a technically competent professional, and then not being able to understand their directions. Developing a good rapport with any professional you hire is critical, in order that a fair and open exchange of ideas takes place between you and your planner. If you do not feel comfortable with the person you are considering as your planner, either address it up front or seek another person for the job. The last section of this chapter, the *Consumer Bill Of Rights for Financial Planning,* provides more detailed information about what to look for, and how to work with a financial planning professional.

Don't be intimidated by any cross-border financial planner, no matter what their reputation or how expensive their fees. Remember he or she is only a person hired by you, to perform a service.

WHAT DOES A CROSS-BORDER FINANCIAL PLAN COST?

Financial planners are compensated by three key methods; by fee only, commission only, or by a combination of fee and commission. If you are dealing with a professional financial planner, they should provide you with a full written disclosure of fees and the method by which they are compensated for their services. If they do not, make certain you ask for it.

Which method of compensation is best for the client is the subject of much debate. In cross-border financial planning, we have found that most clients prefer a fee only basis. They find it reassuring to know that they do not have to buy any financial products to get the necessary advice, and that there are no hidden costs or motives. Since other cross-border financial planning team members such as accountants and attorneys are usually compensated by fees, there is usually a better rapport between the team members, if the financial planner/team leader is paid the same way.

Regardless of how you pay for your cross-border financial plan, a good general rule is, you get what you pay for. A budget plan could get you budget results, and may end up costing you thousands of dollars more in lost benefits, higher than necessary taxes, and poor investment results. Cross-border financial planning is much too complex an endeavor, to take chances by cutting corners.

You can expect a cross-border financial plan from an experienced fee only planner, to cost a minimum of $2,000. Depending on the size and complexity of your estate, some plans can cost upwards to $50,000 and be worth every penny of it. A complete cross-border financial plan takes from 50 to 100 man-hours to complete, and will be comprised of 50 to 60 pages of analysis and recommendations.

Some cross-border financial planners will guarantee that their work will achieve tax or other savings in excess of their fees, or their fees will be partially or fully refundable. Ask for this type of a commitment from your chosen cross-border financial planner.

The highest paid member of the financial planning team should be the one that can save you the most money, and in most cases that will be the team leader/cross-border financial planner.

A CONSUMER BILL OF RIGHTS FOR FINANCIAL PLANNING*

As a consumer, you have a right to know. Whether you are just investigating your options, or have already engaged a financial planner, knowing your rights will help ensure that you have a successful working relationship with a competent, trustworthy financial planner, who can help you achieve financial independence.

Article I

You have the right to receive competent financial advice from a qualified, knowledgeable professional, with financial training, education and experience. Look for a person who has at least one of the following educational credentials:

•A designation in the U.S. such as Certified Financial Planner (CFP), Chartered Financial Consultant (ChFC), Certified Public Accountant (CPA) or Chartered Financial Analyst (CFA). In Canada look for the Chartered Financial Planner (CFP), Registered Financial (RFP) or Chartered Accountant (CA).

•A law degree (JD) in the U.S. or (LL.B. or LL.M.) in Canada.

•A bachelor's or graduate degree in financial planning, money management or related business from an accredited institution.

•Ask about a planner's continuing education activities. Ensure that financial planning is their primary — not part-time job.

Article II

You have the right to work with a planner who is registered as an investment advisor with the Securities and Exchange Commission (SEC), registered with a state agency, and who is licensed to sell investments and insurance, where applicable.

It is important to know if the planner is registered in the U.S. as an investment advisor, because that is the minimum step a planner can take to comply with regulatory requirements. A planner must be licensed with the National Association of Securities Dealers (NASD) and appropriate state insurance departments to sell investments and insurance. In Canada, provincial registration and licensing is required to sell these products.

Article III

You have the right to receive references from the planner. Ask for names and phone numbers of clients whom the planner has worked with, as well as other financial service professionals.

Article IV

You have the right to receive financial planning advice that is tailored to your financial needs. Look for a planner who prepares a financial plan based on the six-step process:

1. Information gathering.

2. Goal setting.

3. Identification of financial problems.

4. Preparation of written recommendations.

5. Implementation of recommendations.

6. Review and revision of the plan.

Ask to see a sample plan to ensure all six steps are included.

Article V

You have the right to receive a financial plan that is cost-effective. The cost to implement the plan should be within your financial means. You also have the right to obtain an estimate of the total costs involved in financial planning from your planner, and to know exactly what services the planner will provide.

Article VI

You have the right to receive from the planner, sufficient information on the risks and benefits of each investment recommended to implement the financial plan.

Make sure the planner explains everything thoroughly, including the "worst-case" and "middle of the road" investment scenarios. You should reject high pressure tactics, and be wary of promises of very high rates of return.

Article VII

You have the right to receive full disclosure about how the planner will be compensated. Inquire about the following four methods of compensation: fee-only, fee-and-commission, commission-only and salary. If you are concerned about conflict of interest in the planner's method of compensation, do not hesitate to ask the planner to explain.

Article VIII

You have the right to receive a full explanation about how the final plan is to be implemented. Ask whether the recommended investments come from one company, or from several different companies. Find out if the planner sells only those products on which they make a commission. And, ask whether the plan can be implemented by buying financial products from other sources.

Article IX

You have the right to receive assurances that the planner has the resources to serve your needs for the next year or more. Find out whether the planner has a network of related professionals — such as tax accountants, attorneys and/or brokers — to consult with you on any special needs that you may have. A good financial planner will pinpoint areas of potential financial difficulty (such as an out dated will) and relate the financial consequences back to you.

Article X

You have the right to receive regular written and verbal updates on the status of your financial plan, and the investments you have made to implement it.

Work with your planner to keep track of your investments on a regular basis. Make sure you understand how your investments are performing. If you are in doubt, keep asking questions.

Reprinted with permission from the Consumer Bill of Rights for Financial Planning, published by the International Association for Financial Planning (IAFP), Atlanta, GA, 1-800-945-IAFP.

LIST OF USEFUL
FREE PUBLICATIONS

United States

All of the following IRS publications are available free of charge at any IRS office, U.S. Embassy, or by calling toll free 1-800-TAX-FORM anywhere in U.S.

#54 Tax Guide for U.S. Citizens and Resident Aliens Abroad

This publication discusses tax situations for U.S. citizens and resident aliens who live and work abroad. In particular, it explains the rules for excluding income and excluding deduction of certain housing costs. Answers are provided to the questions that taxpayers abroad most often ask.

Forms 2555, 1116 and 1040, Schedule SE (Form 1040).

#513 Tax Information for Visitors to the United States

This publication briefly reviews the general requirements of U.S. income tax laws for foreign visitors. You may have to file a U.S. tax return during your visit. Most visitors, who come to the United States are not allowed to work in the United States. Check with the Immigration and Naturalization Service before you take a job.

Forms 1040C, 1040NR, 2063, and 1040-ES(NR).

#514 Foreign Tax Credit for Individuals

This publication may help you if you paid foreign income tax. You may be able to take a foreign tax credit or deduction to avoid the burden of double taxation. The publication explains which foreign taxes qualify, and how to figure your credit or deduction.

Form 1116

#515 Withholding of Tax on Non-Resident Aliens & Foreign Corp.

This publication provides information for withholding agents, who are required to withhold and report tax on payments to non-resident aliens and foreign corporations. Included are three tables listing U.S. tax treaties, and some of the treaty provisions that provide for certain types of income.

Forms 1042 and 1042S, 1001, 4224, 8233, 1078, 8288, 8288-A, 8288-B, 8804, 8805, and W-8, 8813, and 8709.

#519 U.S. Tax Guide for Aliens

This publication gives guidelines on determining your U.S. tax status, and calculating your U.S. tax. Resident aliens, like U.S. citizens, are generally taxed on income from all sources. Non-resident aliens are generally taxed only on income from U.S. sources. The income may be from investments, or from business activities, such as performing personal services in the United States. An income tax treaty may reduce the standard 30% tax rate on non-resident aliens' investment income. Their business income is taxed at the same graduated rates that apply to U.S. citizens or residents.

Aliens admitted to the United States with permanent immigrant visas are resident aliens, while temporary visitors generally are non-resident aliens. Aliens with other types of visas, may be resident aliens or non-resident aliens, depending on the length and nature of their stay.

Forms 1040, 1040C, 1040NR, 2063, and Schedule A (Form 1040).

#593 Tax Highlights for U.S. Citizens & Residents Going Abroad

This publication briefly reviews various U.S. tax provisions that apply to U.S. citizens or resident aliens, who live or work abroad and expect to receive income from foreign sources.

#1581 Foreign Investment in U.S. Real Property

This publication explains the tax consequences of a sale of U.S. property by a non-resident alien owner.

Form 1040NR, Schedule D (Form 1040), 4797, 6251, 8228, and 8288B.

Free Tax Publications Available From Revenue Canada

- Capital Gains Tax Guide
- Pension and RRSP Tax Guide
- Tax Guide for Canadians Living in other Countries
- Tax Guide for Emigrants

Revenue Canada Interpretation Bulletins

IT-29	United States social security tax and benefits
IT-31	Foreign exchange profits and losses
IT-76R2	Exempt portion of pension when employee has been a non-resident
IT-161R3	Non-residents — Exemption from tax deductions at source on employment income
IT-163R2	Election by non-resident individuals on Certain Canadian source income
IT-171R	Non-resident individuals - Taxable income earned in Canada
IT-181	Foreign-tax credit — Foreign-tax carry over
IT-194	Foreign tax credit — Part-time residents
IT-221R2	Determination of an individual's residence status
IT-262R	Losses of non-residents and part-year residents
IT-270R2	Foreign tax credit
IT-298	Canada-U.S. Tax Convention — Number of days "present" in Canada
IT-370	Trusts - Capital property owned on December 31, 1971
IT-372R	Trusts - Flow-through of taxable dividends and interest to a beneficiary (1987 and prior taxation years)
IT-395R	Foreign tax credit — Foreign-source capital gains and losses
IT-399	Principal residence — Rental non-resident owner
IT-420R2	Non-residents — Income earned in Canada
IT-465R	Non-resident beneficiaries of trusts
IT-506	Foreign income taxes as a deduction from income
IT-520	Unused foreign tax credits — Carry forward and carry back

PROVINCIAL AND STATE
TAX RATES

1992 Canadian Provincial Tax Rates

In the wake of provincial budgets, new tax rates are now in effect. Here is what you pay as a percentage of your federal tax. The table does not include the provincial surtaxes that are applied to higher incomes in some provinces.

Newfoundland	64.5*
Prince Edward Island	59.5*
Nova Scotia	59.5
New Brunswick	60.0
Quebec	**
Ontario	54.5*
Manitoba	52.0
Saskatchewan	60.0*
Alberta	46.0*
British Columbia	52.0*
Northwest Territories	44.0
Yukon	45.0

*new this year
** Provincial tax is 16-24% of total income.

Source: CCH Canadian Tax Reporter

Sunbelt State Individual Income Taxes

The following is a summary of state income taxes in popular Sunbelt states, to which individuals may be subject. It is not our intention to provide detailed information with respect to the taxation system of each particular state. The state income tax laws summarized herein are those in effect for the 1991 taxation year.

Arizona — Individuals Liable to Taxation

Residents of Arizona are taxed on all income, whereas non-residents are taxed only on Arizona-source income. A non-resident's taxable income does not include income from intangibles (interest, dividends, etc.) unless derived from a trade or business carried on in the state.

Allowable Deductions

Taxpayers are allowed the standard deduction. In lieu of the standard deduction, taxpayers can elect to use the revised itemized deductions. Deductions allowable under Arizona law are similar to those allowable for federal tax purposes. You must itemize on the federal return (Form 1040 only) to itemize for Arizona purposes.

Rates for Married Filing Jointly or Head of Household

From	To	Tax Rate
0	20,000	3.80%
20,001	50,000	4.40%
50,001	100,000	5.25%
100,001	300,000	6.50%
300,001	Over	7.00%

All taxpayers are allowed credits for taxes paid to other states or Canada.

California — Individuals Liable to Taxation

Residents of California are taxed on taxable income (AGI minus either the itemized or standard deduction). Non-residents and part-year residents are also taxed on taxable income, but their California tax liability is determined based on the ratio of California AGI to worldwide AGI, multiplied by the California tax on worldwide income. A non-resident's AGI does not include income from intangibles (interest, dividends, gains from sales of securities etc.) unless property has a business situs in the state.

California is a community property state. If a married couple is domiciled in California, one half of the community income earned by one spouse is legally owned by, and taxable to the other spouse.

Allowable Deductions

Deductions allowable under California law are similar to the allowable for federal purposes, except that state income taxes are not deductible. Federal income tax is also not deductible. In lieu of itemized deductions, single and married taxpayers may claim standard deductions of $2,262 and $4,514 respectively.

Rates for Married Filing Jointly

From	To	Tax Rate
0	8,788	1.0%
8,789	20,828	2.0%
20,829	32,870	4.0%
32,871	45,632	6.0%
45,633	57,670	8.0%
57,671	200,000	9.3%
200,001	400,000	10.0%
400,001	Over	11.0%

Rates for heads of households range from 1% on the first $8,789 to 11 percent on income over $272,230. For others, the rate on the first $4,394 is 1%, and on income over $200,000 it is 11 per cent. California has an 8.5 per cent alternative minimum tax (AMT). All taxpayers are allowed credit for taxes paid to other states.

Florida — Individuals Liable to Taxation

No individual income tax is imposed by Florida.

Hawaii — Individuals Liable to Taxation

Residents of Hawaii are taxed on their gross income, whereas non-residents are taxed only on their Hawaii-source income. A non-resident's taxable income does not include income from intangibles (interest, dividends, etc.) unless derived from a trade or business carried on in the state.

Allowable Deductions

Deductions allowable under Hawaii law are similar to those allowable for federal income tax purposes.

State income taxes are deductible but federal income taxes are not. Non-residents must allocate their itemized deductions based on the ratio of Hawaii AGI to total AGI.

Rates for Married Filing Jointly

From	To	Tax Rate
0	3,000	2.00%
3,001	5,000	4.00%
5,001	7,000	6.00%
7,001	11,000	7.25%
11,001	21,000	8.00%
21,001	31,000	8.75%
31,001	41,000	9.50%
41,000	Over	10.00%

Special rate tables are provided for other filing statuses. Credit is given only to residents for taxes paid to other states.

Source: CCH State Tax Handbook

CANADIAN EMBASSY & CONSULATES IN THE U.S.

Canadian Embassy
501 Pennsylvania Avenue N.W.
Washington, D.C. 20001
1-800-456-0000

Atlanta - Consulate General of Canada
1 CNN Center
Suite 400, South Tower
Atlanta, Georgia 30303-2705
(404)577-6810 1-800-467-0000

Boston - Consulate General of Canada
3 Copley Place, Suite 400
Boston, MA 02116
1-800-468-0000

Buffalo - Canadian Consulate
1 Marine Midland Centre
Suite 3550
Buffalo, New York 14203-2884
1-800-469-0000

Chicago - Consulate General of Canada
310 South Michigan Avenue, Suite 1200
Chicago, Illinois 60604-4295
1-800-470-0000

Cleveland - Canadian Consulate
Illuminating Building
55 Public Square
Cleveland, Ohio 44113-1983
1-800-471-0000

Dallas - Consulate General of Canada
St. Paul Place, Suite 1700
750 North St. Paul
Dallas, Texas 75201
1-800-472-0000

Detroit - Consulate General of Canada
600 Renaissance Center, Suite 1100
Detroit, Michigan 48243-1704
1-800-473-0000

Los Angeles - Consulate General of Canada
300 S. Grand Avenue
10th Floor, Suite 1000
Los Angeles, CA 90071
(213)687-7432 1-800-476-0000

Minneapolis - Consulate General of Canada
701 - 4th Avenue South
Suite 900
Minneapolis, Minnesota 55415-1899
1-800-474-0000

New York - Consulate General of Canada
1251 Avenue of the Americas
16th Floor
New York, NY 10020-1175
1-800-457-0000

Seattle - Consulate General of Canada
412 Plaza 600
Sixth and Stewart Streets
Seattle, Washington 98101-1286
1-800-477-0000

APPENDIX D

U.S. CONSULATES IN CANADA

Calgary
615 McLeod Trail South
Suite 1000
Calgary, Alberta T2G 4T8
(403)266-8962

Halifax
Suite 910, Cogswell Tower
Halifax, Nova Scotia B3M 4G9
(902)429-2480

Montreal
1155 St. Alexandre St.
Montreal, Quebec H2Z 1Z2
(514)398-9695
P.O. Box 65 Postal Station Desjardins
Montreal, Quebec H5B 1G1

U.S. Consulate General U.S. Mailing Address
Box 847
Champlain, NY 12919

Ottawa
100 Wellington Street
Ottawa, Ontario Canada K1P 5T1
(613)238-5335 Ext. 301

APO/FPO U.S. Mailing Address
P.O. Box 5000
Ogdensburg, NY 13669-0430

Quebec City
2 Place Terrasse Dufferin C.P. 939
Quebec G1R 4T9
(418)692-2095

APO/FPO U.S. Mailing Address
P.O. Box 1545
Champlain, NY 12919-1547

Toronto
360 University Avenue
Toronto, Ontario M5G 1S4
(416)595-0228

APO/FPO U.S. Mailing Address
P.O. Box 135
Lewiston, NY 14092-0135

Vancouver
1095 W. Pender Street
Vancouver, BC V6E 2M6
(604)685-4311

APO/FPO U.S. Mailing Address
Box 5002
Pt. Roberts, Washington 98281

U.S. Embassy In Canada
United States Embassy
100 Wellington Street
Ottawa, Ontario K1P 5T1
(613)238-4470

CANADIAN NEWSPAPERS
AND NEWS LETTERS IN THE U.S.

Canadian Newspapers

The Canada News
P.O. Box 1729
Auburndale, FL, 33823-1729
(813)967-6450 1-800-535-6788

The Sun Times Of Canada
515 West Bay Street
Tampa, FL 33606
1-800-253-4323

Canadian Financial Newsletters in the U.S.

Sunbelt Canadian
4645 N. 32 Street, Suite A-125
Phoenix, AZ 85018
1-800-678-5007

The Brunton U.S. Non-Resident Taxletter
4710 N.W. Boca Raton Blvd, #101
Boca Raton, FL 33431
(407)241-9991

PRIVATE TRAVEL INSURANCE CARRIERS

Nomad Travel Protection
(Offered through John Ingle Travel Insurance)

800 Bay Street
Toronto, ON M5S 3A9
(416)961-0666
1-800-387-4770

Vancouver .... (604)684-0666	Hamilton .... (416)336-2666
Calgary .... (403)236-1666	All Canada 1-800-387-4770
Winnipeg .... (204)694-0666	B.C. & Alberta . 1-800-663-9710
Ottawa .... (613)564-0666	Manitoba 1-800-465-9742
London .... (519)434-0666	Quebec 1-800-363-6710
Mississauga .... (416)275-0666	Atl. Can. 1-800-665-0666
Oshawa .... (416)436-0666	All USA............. 1-800-525-0666
Montreal .... (514)281-0666	Fort Lauderdale (305)561-8666
Halifax .... (902)422-0666	

The Canadian Automobile Association

Travel insurance may be purchased through any Canadian Automobile Association office in Canada. Individual Clubs offer a variety of Out of Canada medical insurance products including Lloyd's of London, Away From Home, and CAARE. For the location of your nearest office consult the white pages of your local directory. Out of province health insurance products are available to both CAA members and non-members.

Voyageur Insurance Company
(Halifax, Montreal, Brampton, Winnipeg, Calgary, Burnaby)

Ontario
44 Peel Centre Drive
Suite 300
Brampton, ON
(416)791-3700

Montreal	(514)871-9139
Halifax	(902)422-1407
Winnipeg	(204)949-0060
Calgary	(403)271-0504
Vancouver	(604)299-7744

Travel Underwriters
(Underwritten by Lloyd's of London, England)

#302 - 5811 Cooney Road
Richmond, BC V6X 3M1
(604) 276-9900

Blue Cross

Quebec Crois Bleue Assurance - Voyage
Case Postale 910, Succursale B
Montreal, PQ H3B 3K8
(514)286-8403

Manitoba Blue Cross
P.O. Box 1046
Winnipeg, MB R3C 2X7
(204)775-0151

Ontario Blue Cross
150 Ferrand Drive
Toronto, ON M3C 1H6
(416)429-2661

Mutual of Omaha Insurance Company of Canada
(Underwritten by Constitution Insurance Company of Canada)

Ontario
500 University Avenue
Toronto, ON M5G 1V8
(416)598-4321

Quebec
50 Cremazie Blvd. West, Room 523
Montreal, PQ H2P 1A7
(514)384-3320

British Columbia
1681 Chestnut Street
Suite 210, Vancouver, BC V6J 4M6
(604)733-9400

Nova Scotia
1526 Dresden Row, Box 3588
South Halifax, NS B3J 3J2
(902)429-6340

Travelwise Insurance Management Inc.
(Underwritten by Reliable Life Insurance Company)
503-287 Broadway
Winnipeg, MB R3C 0R9
(204)942-9473

Travel Insurance Co-ordinators Agencies Ltd.
2467 Bellevue Avenue, P.O. Box 91189
West Vancouver, BC V7V 3N6
(604)926-7779

Travelrite Travel Insurance
(Underwritten by Zurich Canada)

Ontario

Zurich Canada
18 King Street East
Toronto, ON M5C 1C4
FAX: (416)594-5946

Assurance - Vie-Desjardins Inc.

Quebec Only

200 Avenue Des Commandeurs
Levis, PQ G6V 6R2

Simply The Best Travel Insurance
(Offered exclusively through Thomas Cook Travel Agencies,
administered by Pottruff & Smith Insurance Brokers Ltd.)

Pottruff & Smith Insurance Brokers Ltd.
4500 Hwy. #7
Woodbridge, ON L4L 4Y7
(416)856-1981

The Co-operators Travel Insurance
(Underwritten by Co-operators General Insurance Company)
Priory Square
Guelph, ON N1H 6P8
(519)824-4400

Travel Health Plan - Maritime Medical Care
7 Spectacle Lake Drive
Dartmouth, NS
P.O. Box 2200
Halifax, NS B3J 3C6
(902)468-9700

Odyssey Travel Insurance

Canadian Insurance Management Inc.
425 Bloor Street East
Toronto, ON M4W 3R5

The Globetrotter Travel Insurance Plan

Laurentian General Insurance Company
2960 Laurier Blvd., Suite 300
P.O. Box 10900
Ste-Foy, PQ G1V 4S8

APPENDIX G

CANADIAN CLUBS IN THE U.S.

Canadian Club of the Desert
P.O. Box 284
Cathedral City, CA 92235

Canadian Social Club of Greater Phoenix
4645 N. 32 Street
Suite A-125
Phoenix, AZ 85018
1-800-678-5007

Canadian Association of Orange County
7444 Calico Trail
Orange, CA 92669

Canadian Society of Southern California
908 Shenandoah Street
Suite 203
Los Angeles, CA 90035

Canadian American Society of the Southeastern United States, Inc.
6472 E. Church Street
Douglasville, GA 30134
(404)920-0617

Canadian Women's Club
2581 Rock Point Lane
Lithonia, GA 30058
(404)979-7675

The Canadian Society of St. Petersburg
370 N. 53rd Ave. #574
St. Petersburg, FL 33703

The Canadian Club of Ocala
19125 SW Glenco Place
Dunnellon, FL 32630

The Canadian Club of Springhills
11038 Upton Street
Springhills, FL 34608

Royal Canadian Legion, Post 144, Pinellas County
3663 N. 58th Avenue, #354
St. Petersburg, FL 33714

Canadian Club
603 W. 63rd Avenue, #T24
Bradenton, FL 34207

Canadian Snowbirds Pensioners
455 Trinadad Lane
Largo, FL 34640

Canadian-American Business Association, Inc.
20 N. Orange Avenue
Suite 1400
Orlando, FL 32801
(305)841-7337

Canadian Franco-American Club of St. Petersburg
6012 N. 68th Avenue
Pinellas Park, FL 33565
(813)546-0601

Daytona Beach Canadian Club
c/o Mr. W. J. Connor
City Island Recreation Hall
Daytona Beach, FL 32016
(904)252-0132

Canadian Club of America, Inc.
352 Davis Road
Palm Springs, FL 33461
(407)967-3054

Canadian Club
304 Boca Ciega Point Blvd. South
Madeira Beach, FL 33461
(813)392-8675

Canadian Society
211 S.E. 1st Avenue
Hallandale, FL 33009

Clearwater Canadian Club
465 Ulmerton Road
Largo, FL 33541
(813)584-1975

Canadian Club of Charlotte County
756 New York Avenue NE
Port Charlotte, FL 33952
(813)625-0132

Canadian Club of Colony Cove
115 Pompano Drive
Ellenton, FL 34222

Canadian Snow Bird Association
P.O. Box 1704
Auburndale, FL 33823
1-800-265-3200

INDEX